DAYS OF FEAR

Daniele Mastrogiacomo

DAYS OF FEAR
A Firsthand Account of Captivity
Under the New Taliban

*Translated from the Italian
by Michael Reynolds*

Europa
editions

Europa Editions
116 East 16th Street
New York, N.Y. 10003
www.europaeditions.com
info@europaeditions.com

Translation by Michael Reynolds
Original Title: *I giorni della paura*

Library of Congress Cataloging in Publication Data is available
ISBN 978-1-933372-97-6

Mastrogiacomo, Daniele
Days of Fear

Book design by Emanuele Ragnisco
www.mekkanografici.com
Cover photograph © Robert Patrick/CORBIS SYGMA

Prepress by Plan.ed – Rome

Printed in Canada

CONTENTS

INTRODUCTION

One is inclined to use the word "Conradian" to describe *Days of Fear*. Daniele Mastrogiacomo is a reporter and this is a work of reportage. It is not fiction. Daniele recounts an ordeal that was lived firsthand. When he describes being flogged by the Taliban he makes us feel the lashes on his skin. He makes us feel them on our skin, too, and we know that his pain and humiliation cannot be the fruit of imagination. They are reality, as real as the blood that flows from the decapitated body of Sayed, pushed into the river to disappear, carried away by the current. And equally real, though Daniele is not in a position to describe it for us, is the fate of Ajmal, the young Tajik, Daniele's interpreter and friend. Daniele believed that Ajmal had made it safely back home. Instead, after a staged liberation, he, too, was assassinated. Daniele was in Italy when he learned of Ajmal's death; he was at home, celebrating the end of his terrible adventure which was now become a superb piece of reporting.

The portrait of the Taliban that Daniele painstakingly composes step by step, day by day, observing them during their insane dashes over the Afghan desert, or during anguishing hours spent in makeshift prisons with his feet and hands bound, has an extremely rare authenticity, one that is not often achieved by journalists, whose profession frequently turns them into voyeurs, removed from events and from their subjects. Daniele's portrait of the Taliban is one that only a prisoner can make, a hostage, a victim, someone who is prey to all the fears that a brush with death of this kind provokes, but who never loses his reporter's gaze. The sinister simplicity of the young Taliban soldiers, suspended between mysticism and cruelty, smiling yet ruthless, like fanatical clerics from some medieval morality tale, is described with a directness that needs no special effects to rivet the reader's attention.

Daniele's account smacks of Conrad because the deaths of Sayed and Ajmal are always looming in the background. Daniele is not Marlow. Daniele is Lord Jim himself. A Lord Jim who speaks to his listeners directly, without intermediaries, modestly allowing the sense of guilt he feels for the deaths of his two companions to seep into his story. Like Lord Jim, Daniele cannot be accused of anything. It was not he who abandoned to their fate his interpreter and driver, collaborators for whom war correspondents have always been honor-bound to take responsibility. There was nothing Daniele could have done for them.

Yet between the lines of his story emerges the moral wound that he still carries and which this book does not in any way attempt to erase. I recall what Conrad wrote in 1917 about his Lord Jim: he was "one of us."

Bernardo Valli, veteran foreign affairs correspondent for Italy's leading daily newspaper, *La Repubblica*
June 2009

DAYS OF FEAR

They affectionately call me the Resurrected One. But it is thanks rather to a series of fortuitous and random circumstances, and to the actions of several men and women that I made it back home alive.

They deserve special thanks and it is to them I dedicate this book.

Luisella Longo Orihuela
Ezio Mauro
Elisabetta Belloni
Massimo D'Alema
Romano Prodi
Gino Strada
Rahmatullah Hanefi

And the ninety thousand people all over the world who signed the appeal for my and Ajmal's release.

Agha Srawiz has no time to make bread today. His young assistants are gathered around a gaping mouth of fire opened in the dirt floor. He sends them home and closes the bakery. It's Wednesday, June 1, 2005. He leaves his shop and walks, his eyes focused on a fixed spot in front of him. When he reaches the great mosque in the center of Kandahar, an Afghan city lying eighty kilometers from the border with Pakistan, it is 9:30 in the morning. Inside the mosque, they are commemorating the death of Mullah Abdul Fayez, former head of the regional Islamic council.

Fayaz had raised his voice in his final sermons. He had roared his disapproval of the Taliban, who were becoming increasingly active in the city, and had thrown his weight against Mullah Mohammed Omar, born and raised in this part of the country, supreme spiritual guide and uncontested leader of the Qur'anic student movement. Three days after what would turn out to be his final speech, Fayaz was killed. A car bomb. Now, they have hastened here to remember him. The upper echelons of the national police are at the ceremony, as is the chief of the Kabul police, Akram Khakrizwal. He has received death threats of late but he's tough as nails and has become hardened to them. Khakrizwal's presence is crucial: the government institutions that emerged out of Afghanistan's first democratic elections must show people that they are here, that they exist. And so he has come. He is in front of his mat, in the first row, praying.

The baker stands in a corner, lost in the crowd of brethren who have not been able to find a spot inside. He waits for the service to end. Chiefs, division heads, and ordinary police officers begin to flood out of the mosque. The man walks over to a disorderly pile of shoes on a mat at the entrance. An accomplice points out the chief of police's black moccasins. The man picks them up and elbows his way through the crowd until he reaches the chief of police. He kneels, kisses the man's hand as a sign of respect and reverence, slips the shoes onto his feet, and pulls a metal ring that triggers a detonator. The belt of TNT he is wearing under his coat explodes. The attack wreaks havoc on the official entourage. The body of the chief of police is pulverized. It is a dramatic act, a bona fide provocation. The entire country is rocked, but shock waves are felt most keenly in the government of Hamid Karzai, the nation's first democratically elected president, which finds itself in an increasingly weak and difficult position.

The following days pass to the rhythm of attacks, dozens of them, in cities all over the country's southern provinces. After four days a group of Taliban claims responsibility for bringing down an American fighter jet in Khost Province—also in the south but on the other side of the country. A DVD with footage of a land-to-air missile striking a military jet bearing the insignia of the US Air Force is sent to an Afghan news agency.

The episode is kept under wraps but colleagues in Kabul call to give me the news. They also send me the short video, which I immediately have analyzed by an expert. He tells me that the footage is real: it hasn't been retouched. My first thought is of Ajmal Naqshbandi, my friend and interpreter. I haven't seen him for a year. I get occasional emails in which he talks about his life and his work. He's a freelance journalist—not an easy thing to be in a country like Afghanistan, where there's plenty of news, but it always seems the same and doesn't interest the foreign press too much.

I decide to call him. This series of attacks is an important sign. Until recently, the Taliban were considered all but vanished, defeated; now they seem to be back. Ambushes, firefights, car bombs—this is how they announce their return. I need confirmation. I want to know if these are symptoms of some type of change, to understand if it is the old mullahs routed out during the international coalition's invasion of Afghanistan who are behind the incidents, or whether new blood is running through the Taliban's veins. Very few people are talking, even fewer are able to gather reliable information. The Qur'anic students live in the shadows, shrouded in mystery. But if I want to continue reporting on Afghanistan I must try to discover how strong they are, how much territory they have under their control, how much influence they wield in southern Afghanistan. Who is paying them, who is training them, who is supporting them? I want to know them better. My profession demands it. My position obligates me to tell the story of this war that the world feels is far away, to measure reality against what passes for reality in the official bulletins from the central command of ISAF, the international coalition under NATO leadership. According to these reports, the resistance posed by the Taliban is weak, almost inevitable, predictable; it is no cause for concern.

The suicide bomber-baker demonstrates that the reality in Afghanistan is different from what the Karzai administration, for reasons of political opportunism, does its utmost to portray. Something big is happening in the country that I first got to know five years back. There is a new and important element: for the first time in the history of Afghanistan, suicide bombers have appeared on the scene. An alien body in the culture of a people made up of fighters who have never submitted to a foreign army in centuries and centuries of bellicose history. I think of the return of the Arab-Afghans, legendary figures grown somewhat pale, held at a distance, viewed suspiciously by the local mujahedeen. They flocked here to join the international jihad brigades during the Taliban offensive towards the end of 1994, at the culmination of the civil war between Ahmed Shah Massoud, Gulbuddin Hematyar, and Abdul Rashid Dostum, the three great leaders of Afghan fighters. Perhaps they're back. My interpreter can help me understand.

I met Ajmal Naqshbandi in November 2001. A Tajik from a middle-class family, he was twenty-three years old and had ties to the Northern Alliance, led by Massoud, the "Lion of Panshir," betrayed and murdered on the eve of the September 11 attack on the Twin Towers. Ajmal had experienced the cruelty of the Shariah firsthand—he'd been found more than once in the wrong place at the wrong time with his beard too short and his hair too long, and had gotten himself arrested. He laughed these episodes off.

And Ajmal laughs now when I ask him if he still sports a goatee and hint at my plans to meet the Qur'anic students. He is overjoyed. In his soft voice, he politely asks me the ritual questions about my life, family, and health, and then says he can't wait to see me. "I wait for you. Like always," he replies when I mention my return to Kabul. "I have many more contacts now," he hastily adds, almost as if he wants to help me to make up my mind. "The others have their merits, but these days I am the only one in all of Afghanistan who can obtain something big with the Taliban. They call me often on the telephone; I have been to places where no one has ever been."

I haven't been to Afghanistan since 2005. I've always had mixed feelings about that country. It fascinates me with its majestic mountain ranges covered in snow almost year-round, its long bumpy roads, its immense valleys, and its mountain peaks that seem to touch the sky. But Afghanistan also inspires unease, almost fear, certainly dread. It is an open-air prison where an estimated ten million landmines scattered throughout thirty-four provinces make free movement impossible, and it oppresses for this reason. An entire country punctuated by death.

Many have helped sow these lethal seeds: mujahedeen, criminals, warlords, Red Army soviets, and western military forces. Over the years, whoever has tried to clean up that hail of explosives has worked with an overwhelming sense of resignation. More than one bomb-disposal expert has told me that there are no up-to-date maps of the antipersonnel mines, and that even many of the outdated ones have now been lost.

I haven't seen Kabul since the kidnapping of Clementina Cantoni, a young Italian volunteer worker with Care International. People who have been there for work tell me that the situation has changed since May 2005. "In many ways," they tell me, "Afghanistan is more dangerous than Iraq."

It's January 2007. I call Ajmal again. I tell him I can't leave for Afghanistan right now, but that the trip has only been postponed. That country is part of me by now; I have many contacts, I've read dozens of books—old publications found at used bookstalls. I tell my Tajik interpreter to move ahead with our project: he must arrange a telephone interview with a Taliban military commander.

"They'll be interested," I explain. "Few people are willing to risk publishing the ideas of the Qur'anic students. But we need to get them on tape in order to understand who they are, how numerous they are, what their plans are. I can imagine their position, they're light years away from the way we see things. But in order to really understand, we need them. And I, we, you, yourself, Ajmal . . . We all need to understand."

My journalist friend wastes no time. A week later he sends me an interview via email with Doctor Ibrahim Hanifi, once tied to Abdul Hai Mutmahin, Information and Culture minister during the reign of the mullahs, the Taliban's spokesman, universally recognized as responsible for the movement's relations with the media. Hanifi is currently serving time after having been arrested in Pakistan on January 17, 2007, and a Taliban death sentence hangs over his head. Among the crimes of which he is accused by the Movement's leaders is his concession of an earlier interview with *La Repubblica* in which he gave a detailed description of the Taliban military structure and the new strategies they are developing. I remember nothing about him or his rather shocking revelations.

The newspaper publishes this second interview, too, and when I talk to Ajmal on the phone he is ecstatic. He says it sent shock waves through the Taliban movement and that he has benefited from its publication. They've contacted him several times; they seek him out, they use him as a conduit with the outside world. They now consider him a trusted contact and he has access to precious sources. He uses this position during the detention of Gabriele Torsello, the freelance photographer captured by a group of criminals on the road between Lashkar Gah and Kandahar, in southwest Afghanistan.

I don't follow the Torsello story. Without an entry visa, I am forced to stay in Rome and then the newspaper sends me to Somalia, where the Islamic Courts Union has been routed by the Ethiopian army, intervening in support of the transitional federal government. Ajmal is a little disappointed. He needed the work my visit would have guaranteed him. He calls every so often to give me news of Torsello's kidnapping, confirming that it is the work of local bandits, and that there is nothing political to it. The Taliban themselves, slighted by an action that gets so much attention and was carried out in a territory that they consider theirs, offer to collaborate in the liberation of the Italian photojournalist.

Ajmal is sure that he can satisfy my request because he has already tested the waters. As it turns out, a week before we are captured by the Taliban, Ajmal will travel to the same area with a colleague from the English-language branch of al-Jazeera. And with another reporter from a private television network in London, Channel Four, he will contact Mullah Dadullah, emerging leader of the military wing of the Taliban, one of the ten members of the Supreme Shura, the executive political branch of the movement led by Mullah Mohammed Omar. He and the English reporter conduct an interview that makes a lot of noise. Ajmal returns to Helmand Province with a French colleague, and, yet again, with three Afghan journalists. He considers himself an expert on the Taliban. But it is with the foreign correspondent from Channel Four that he gets his biggest scoop. "There are three thousand suicide bombers ready to blow themselves up here in Afghanistan," announces Dadullah, a commander who is known to be as rebellious towards the leadership of the Qur'anic student movement as he is ruthless with his victims. Concerning the legend that has been circulating throughout Afghanistan for years, Dadullah reveals the following: "Bin Laden is alive. We don't see him, but we are in contact with him. He is ready to act; he is studying a new strategy with us. He follows our developments and advises us."

The international press, including *La Repubblica*, picks up the story the following day. I write a brief piece for the foreign news section. The Taliban will talk to me often about this interview during our days of captivity: they considered it the only interview, among the countless others given but never aired or published, that faithfully reflected the ideas of the military commander of Helmand Province.

G oing to Afghanistan is not a trip, it is an adventure. You have to prepare physically and mentally, you have to think carefully about your luggage and the clothes you bring; what objects, books, documentation to take with you, and how much money to carry. You have to understand and predict the weather and think through what you'll be doing and where you'll be going. A bona fide mission that obliges me to undertake a special psychological ritual every time I go.

To this day Afghanistan remains a country I cannot fathom. I can't understand it, enter into its spirit, experience it to any real depth. It is foreign to me, it escapes my sensibility. There is something lacking in the relationship between me, both as a man and as a journalist, and that vast, mysterious, hostile country scarred by war, vendettas, misery, death, and desperation. I have never felt that connection we all search for with the places we visit.

I know I have to leave, and as soon possible. February 26 is a Monday. I wake early and present myself at the Afghan Embassy in via Nomentana, Rome, with a visa request in my hand. I tell the consular official that I need a visa now. I insist, but every effort to explain proves useless: I will have to wait the mandatory five days before they grant me a visa. Nonetheless, they tell me to come back tomorrow.

I'm anxious, the piece cannot be delayed. Indeed, that

morning I am awoken by important news from Afghanistan: a car full of TNT careened into the main entrance of the military base in Bagram, fifty kilometers north of Kabul, massacring countless Afghan citizens on their way to work. It is not a routine attack. It signals a new level of conflict, the deadly vanguard of an offensive that the Taliban officially announced would begin with the first days of spring, when the snows melt and the high mountain passes are once again accessible. The car bomb was meant for the American Vice President, Dick Cheney, who had arrived in Afghanistan the night before on a visit shrouded in secrecy. He had come in from Islamabad, Pakistan, where he met with Pervez Musharraf. It had been a tense meeting, during which the vice president intimated that Pakistan must take more effective measures to combat the Taliban, who circulate freely in the tribal zones on the border between Pakistan and Afghanistan. Cheney had resorted to a bit of characteristically American pragmatism: he threatened to turn off the faucet, to block the eighty million dollars in aid that the Bush administration provides annually to one of its most solid allies in the region.

Relationships between America and Pakistan have always vacillated between threats and flattery, declarations of esteem and shocking ruptures. But this meeting signaled a new crisis in their relations to which Musharraf was forced to respond in the only way possible: obtaining results on the ground, moving troops to the border, capturing, hindering, and laying siege to the Taliban. The Pakistani president takes firm action, getting the results that America has long been waiting for. And he does so in a way that makes waves: a wholesale blitz on a hotel in Quetta, in the extreme northwest of the country. Mullah Obaidullah, former minister of Defense during the Taliban regime, is taken prisoner. The news is kept secret, but, naturally, it doesn't go unnoticed by the intelligence apparatus of the Qur'anic student movement—an information network whose efficiency and knack for infiltrating official Afghan intelligence I learned to appreciate during our captivity.

The reaction, an act of naked revenge, comes within twenty-four hours: the car bomb in Bagram. Very few people knew about Cheney's visit to Kabul. And even fewer knew that he had cancelled his meeting with Afghan president, Hamid Karzai, at the last minute because of a snowstorm that forced him to stay on the Bagram military base, run by US forces since 2001.

The American vice president is unharmed. He was sleeping safely while the carnage was loosed upon the population outside. But the attack means that I have to get to Afghanistan as soon as possible—now! The country is going up in flames much faster than any of the experts predicted.

My captors will repeatedly ask me if Vice President Cheney is dead. They have no idea he was not harmed, and they suspect the usual work of misinformation on the part of the international press, all on the payroll, they say, of the western propaganda machine.

I'm held up for three hours at the Afghan Embassy. Assailed by the usual anxiety, my bags packed and ready but sitting at home, the final details still to be sorted out, and my cell phone glowing hot with calls from the editorial offices of my newspaper asking if I'm going to make my plane. The march of time is inexorable, trampling the minutes underfoot.

I don't know if it was destiny announcing itself via these signals. But I feel them weighing on me. They annoy me, they are like those obstacles that delay us during our evening commute, when we are eager to burrow ourselves away at home and enjoy a little calm and quiet.

But I don't see them as something that fate, or anything or anyone else inhabiting some higher plain of existence, is sending me under the guise of obscure premonitions. In the final equation, I am about to leave on one of the many journeys that my profession affords me. I'm going to a country that I know well, where I'll be able to get things done as if I were a local.

After what seems like an infinite wait, the consular official stamps my passport with an entry visa and distractedly hands it back to me. The ride to Fiumicino airport is an insane race against time. Luckily, my taxi driver is a specialist in mad dashes and he gets me to the terminal in time. I am duly greeted by smiling check-in personnel at the Emirates Airlines counter. The importunities of fate, all the obstacles thrown in my path, seem to lose their strength. Everything returns to its proper and natural course. As is always the case.

I sleep long and deeply during the flight to Dubai, and then again in the small hotel where I am a guest for a few short hours while waiting for my connecting flight to Afghanistan. All goes well and I arrive, on time, at Kabul International Airport.

My interpreter, Ajmal, is waiting for me outside. He looks happy, satisfied. But I notice right away that he has changed: his eyes are older; a few wrinkles have hardened his round face. He is quiet, engrossed in his own thoughts. He has never really opened up and confided in me—he is reticent and discreet by nature. But he now looks more hermetic than ever, like he's hiding things. His family is always complaining about the same thing: he doesn't tell them what he does, or where he goes, or with whom. His philosophy has always been to say as little as possible in order to protect himself and those who are closest to him.

He's put on a few kilos too many. He touches the "spare tire" around his waist, and sighs: "I have to lose some weight. Marriage is good for the spirit, but not for the body." So, he finally got married. A girl of seventeen. He had known her for three years and every two weeks, on Friday morning, he would go to visit her in Logar Province, south of Kabul. I've never met her, he's never told me her name. I know only that she's from a well-to-do, influential family and that her father is a famous surgeon. My interpreter had to win her family over one day at a time, finally obtaining their consent for the union, a matter that is always decided by the patriarchs of the families concerned.

Ajmal announces that his older brother, Lehmar, with whom he had once run the Everest Guest House in the center of Kabul—where I stayed for many months and which has now been returned to its Tehran owners—has left Afghanistan. He makes no mention of Taliban threats. I will learn about these only after my release, when Lehmar himself tells me the whole story. All Ajmal says is that the plans they had in mind never worked out. First a small hotel, then a restaurant, they even tried to run a gas station equipped with an automatic car wash. But none of these projects got off the ground. Lehmar chose to emigrate. He was granted political asylum in Belgium, where he is now waiting on a job, slowly and with great difficulty adapting to his new home. I ask for more news about Lehmar, whom I remember as a composed person, but Ajmal changes the subject, bringing the conversation back to himself. He says he's unhappy, that he's had to bear all the responsibility, not to mention the economic and psychological burden of his family—in addition to his parents, he has two sisters and three brothers. He still has a special relationship with his mother, whom he adores, and with his little sister, a child of ten. Their closeness is palpable. When he talks about her his eyes grow large and fill with pride. "She is my joy," he confirms. Then, worried, he explains, "I have to take care of everything. The little one's school, her friends, her whims. I had to give Lehmar, over there in Belgium, all my savings. I have to take care of another brother, Munir. He can't stand on his own two feet yet but he's planning on making a future in information technologies. Then, there's my mother, who's always asking me for money."

Ajmal shakes his head. I look at him, respectful of this pause. Then, still looking straight ahead, he starts talking again. He now drives an old Toyota Corolla. "You can see, can't you?" he continues. "I had to rent out my truck. I have to do a thousand jobs, and I hardly have any time to devote to journalism. Every time I visit my parents they're waiting for me impatiently because they know I'm the only one who brings home any money. If I tell them I don't have any, my mother sulks in silence and starts crying. I know, it's emotional blackmail and I hate it; it's wrong and unfair. My wife always says the same thing. But there's nothing else I can do. My father works for Ariana airlines as a technician. But he pockets his pay and never pulls it out. He sacrificed a lot for us children—we never went without during the hard years of the civil war. Meat two times a week, fresh bread every day. He makes it clear that now it's our turn. But the weight of everything, the real responsibility for the family, falls entirely to me."

I listen to him as he vents his frustration. Ajmal needs to talk and to voice his concerns. When, finally, it's quiet inside the Corolla I look outside. Kabul seems different: more modern, more orderly. It is overrun by frenetic activity, by business that transforms it a little more each day. Modern buildings, skyscrapers, shopping malls made of glass and cement. And then, the big hotel, the Serena in the center of Kabul, a few steps from the Blue Mosque, built to the tune of millions by the prince, Aga Khan.

We first stop by the offices of Ariana airlines. I want to buy our tickets for Kandahar right away and check the departure times. We learn that there is only one flight a week, on Saturdays. We reserve two seats—there will be time enough over the following days to buy the tickets.

We are back out on the street. It has rained and there is mud everywhere. My shoes have lost all their color. Ajmal's, on the other hand, black moccasins with thick soles, extremely popular among Afghans, are like new. We head in the direction of the hotel my newspaper booked for me. My interpreter starts to joke around. A light black beard that ends in a pointed goatee frames his face. He strokes it and looks over at me, bemused. He's reminding me of the pact we made years ago. We'll let our beards grow this time as well. It will be necessary, especially in my case, to mask my decidedly western appearance, the color of my hair, my eyes, and my face. "You never change," adds Ajmal good-humoredly as he slaps my shoulder. "You look just like an American."

This fact is not encouraging. To be singled out as American, or English, or Dutch, one of the foreigners serving in the coalition forces, rouses too many suspicions. Afghans respect you, but the way they look at you betrays an easily understandable hostility. They feel they have been invaded. Protected by soldiers who incessantly patrol the center of town and the outlying suburbs, but also oppressed by a presence that they tolerate with great difficulty. I have noticed the same thing in every country in which foreign troops are present, from Iraq to Somalia.

As we bounce over the craters that open before us along the road, I ask Ajmal the question that has been haunting me for five months: Why haven't the Karzai administration and the coalition paved the Jalalabad road? It is a large artery that connects Kabul to Peshawar, in Pakistan, along which thousands of semis and hundreds of foreign military vehicles travel. But there it is, perpetually in ruins, left to its own devices, devastated by truck wheels and tank treads that devour the earth and dig potholes that fill with water and mud.

Ajmal has no answer to my question. He smiles, because it's a question that I ask him every time we see each other. I am convinced that even via these kinds of simple but vital measures a relationship based on trust can be built with a population that has never tolerated the presence of foreign armies on its soil.

I check into my room, open the window and am immediately assailed by a dense smoke, acrid and bluish: car and truck pollution squats over the entire city like a low fog. Kabul is suffering from its leap towards modernity. It willingly accepts the advantages offered by the rich and opulent West, but it advances blindly, unable to keep pace. More often than not, it buckles under the weight of the changes, and it grasps desperately at rituals, customs, and sentiments belonging to a tradition that is slowly disappearing. Traffic is a problem, an environmental emergency, as are space heaters, which, despite bans, the Afghans insist on fueling with diesel.

West and East, a love-hate relationship, cultures that are different but interdependent, struggling to co-exist.

Ajmal and I make an appointment for later that afternoon and he leaves me in my room. He has to take care of a few things, confirm the final details of our trip to Kandahar and Lashkar Gah, and organize the timing and the format of the interview. It's Wednesday, we have only a few days. We need to confirm our flight reservation and call the hotel, the only safe one in Kandahar, where we'll be spending a night. I call my embassy and ask for Ettore Sequi, whose long experience as a diplomat I have had occasion to appreciate over the years. He's not in, but I leave my cell number and a message to say I'm in Afghanistan. I am not nervous about our plans. On the contrary, I feel calm, for Ajmal seems serene, untroubled, sure of what he has done and will do.

I spend this morning, like every morning, reading. It distracts and relaxes me, carrying me away to far-off lands. I read continually: books on Afghanistan, on Central Asia. I've brought with me all the works of Ahmed Rashid, the Pakistani journalist who introduced me to the world of the Qur'anic students. I reread what he wrote about the Taliban during their offensive.

The Great Game by Peter Hopkirk—the story of the perennial struggle between England and Russia for control of a country that offered them nothing. Philip Roth's most recent literary effort. And my old and worn edition of *The Plague*, which accompanies me like a lucky charm on every trip I make. Albert Camus is the only writer capable of conveying the real atmosphere of the places he describes, even down to their smells.

The front desk calls: Ajmal has arrived. He's waiting in the lobby of the Serena. From the window I see and smell nothing but city traffic. Everything is covered in dust that rises from streets stripped of their asphalt, covered in dirt that will turn to mud with the first rains, lined with drainage ditches carrying waste from the houses.

Sewer stench filters into my room and forces me to spray deodorant all over, even on the air conditioner outlet.

The Serena is a sumptuous hotel in the Oriental style with large rooms that are almost always being used for conventions, meetings of various kinds, and summits between the Afghan army, ISAF forces, and NATO. There are two restaurants: the classic bistro, with meals arranged circularly inside warmed aluminum containers, suitable for quick snacks and the big brunches held every Friday, the day of rest in Muslim countries; and a Japanese restaurant that even manages to put sushi—a rarity in a landlocked country hemmed in by mountains—on its menu a couple of times a week. The hotel is a kind of bunker. The cement barricades serve to remind everyone of this fact, especially the dappled crowds hanging about beyond them, or circulating in the central bazaar: merchants, artisans, beggars, mutilated and crippled victims of the antipersonnel mines.

Ajmal and I order tea in a small private room in the back of the hotel. We discuss the details of our journey southwards, into the Taliban stronghold. He says everything is ready, the interview has been arranged.

That evening I reach him on his cell phone at the new home he shares with his young wife and ask him for more information: the name of the commander we'll be interviewing and the faction to which he belongs. Ajmal's answers are vague. It isn't clear if he wants to protect his sources or needs time to nail down the final details. I trust him, exactly as I have trusted him in the five years that we've known one another, during which our work together has always gone off without a hitch, without any blunders or setbacks.

We meet again the following day and go to purchase our tickets. Then, we make a quick visit to the Italian military base, Camp Invicta, thirty kilometers south of Kabul. Finally, we go to the market to get my *shalwar kameez*, a traditional outfit comprised of loose trousers under a long tunic open along the sides.

I don't sport this dress to camouflage myself, but out of respect for local customs. When one is a guest in another's house it is considered polite to wear a *shalwar*. Ajmal himself has requested I do so. I choose an electric blue cap called a *pakol* that matches my *patu*, a long shawl one wears either over the shoulder or wound around one's head like a turban.

On Saturday, March 3, we get up early. The small twin-engine plane connecting Kabul to Kandahar leaves at eleven, but it's best to get to the international airfield two hours early. Ajmal's younger brother takes us there. Aimal has the same wide face as Ajmal and their older brother, Lehmar, the only two members of the family I have met. They seem to have been cast with the same mold, nearly clones. I leave my bags full of clothes in Ajmal's care and I take charge of the equipment: the GPS, the BGAN antenna—a device that opens like a book and allows you to make a broadband internet connection anywhere—my PC, the small video camera that my colleagues at *La Repubblica* entrusted to me. My report on the Taliban is a big opportunity for everyone. Even the images I've started to collect while in Kabul might be useful as fresh material for stories on Afghanistan.

It has snowed overnight, and this morning the flakes are still coming down, getting heavier all the time. I am starting to fear that the flight may be cancelled. This kind of thing happens all the time in Kabul, particularly during the winter, when it can sometimes snow for five days straight. We take cover in a small bar located outside the airport: a large room with a sheet-metal roof where travelers, crowding together to keep warm, wait for their flights while sipping tea and eating scrambled eggs and meat and tomato croquettes.

We wait for three hours. The snow is still falling at noon, when an airline employee responsible for ingress into the airport bursts into the room and announces that the flight for Kandahar has been cancelled. We go back to the hotel. I'm disappointed. There will be more difficulties, I think, further obstacles. Ajmal reassures me. He says that the flight will leave tomorrow, that it's only a short delay. I'm worried about our appointment and afraid that the interview is about to evaporate into thin air. "The Taliban sure aren't going to wait until it stops snowing," I remark. "Perhaps we should give up." My interpreter doesn't reply. His gaze, however, is troubled. I shut myself away in the hotel and ask him if we can meet later in the afternoon.

Ajmal arrives on time, like always, and we drink tea. We talk about his latest jobs and he tells me about a voyage he made to Kunar, in the east. "Al-Qaeda's men," he says, "the famous Arab-Afghans, are dug in over there. They're hiding in a part of the country that I had no idea even existed: an exceptional area, both for the strategic advantages it offers and for its natural beauty: an impenetrable forest that covers the entire side of a mountain. To get there you have to walk for eight hours—serious trekking, you have to be fit. I did it, but it was tough. My companion was forced to give up." I ask him who his companion was and he utters the same name I have heard many times during our telephone conversations over the past few months. "Claudio Franco, my friend the freelance reporter. He's Italian but he lives in London. We went together to Kunar," he explains, his eyes shining with pride and satisfaction. "They even shot at us," he adds. "A rocket. Lucky for us it missed. It hit a rocky outcrop behind us, right as we were heading into a curve."

I am dumbstruck. The Mujahedeen's reaction was over the top, to say the least, and I can't understand why. But Ajmal, still smiling, says that Afghanistan is precisely this: one giant civil war that drags on forever. He adds that it was a mistake on their part. The rebels—that's what they call them—are always suspicious. He tells me that he stayed in the area after finding someone to take his friend back to Kabul. "I wandered around on foot for seven days straight," he recalls. "But in the end I made contact with them again. I explained exactly who I was and what I was doing there. At that point they apologized and agreed to meet me. They consider themselves at war: it's understandable that they react instinctively like that." Naturally, he didn't meet any al-Qaeda terrorists. "They stay deep in the forest, near their training camp. I met with an emissary midway, in a mountain cabin, where I slept for a while as I waited for nightfall, the only time I could move."

His stories fascinate me and at the same time they scare me. I am convinced that Ajmal does indeed have good contacts, but I distrust the indecisive, wavering behavior of the insurgents. I'm puzzled by it. I tell him so and we discuss the question at length. The situation in Afghanistan has degenerated much more that I had imagined. My interpreter listens to my opinions, considers the ifs, ands, and buts aloud, and recites every detail of our journey and the arrangements he's made, listing the names of the sources and the various spokesmen whom he has contacted about the interview.

He demonstrates a deep knowledge of the area we're heading to and of the power relationships between the various Taliban factions. His experience comforts me. He has prepared the meeting with the Taliban military commander down to the smallest detail. He now tells me the name of the interviewee: Mullah Dadullah, emerging leader and commander of Helmand Province. We fix an appointment for the following day and say goodbye.

I wake at dawn and go downstairs to breakfast. Through the window I see that it is still snowing. I shake my head. I'm angry. The flight for Kandahar will be cancelled again. When I call Ajmal, he's still sleeping. He had a bad night, he says. His wife slipped while taking a shower and injured her face and head. Ajmal had to take her to the hospital, where they gave her stitches. He's worried but he's not about to pull out of the trip. The flight, he says, has been confirmed. He called the head of the control tower directly.

I go back to my room and put on my traditional attire for the first time. It fits to a tee, and I feel perfectly at ease. Ajmal arrives, comes straight up to my room, and after a few minutes we leave. In the corridor, some Italian colleagues ask where I'm going. I don't give them any clear answers, hinting at the south. They don't comment, but their interpreter tries to get a few details out of Ajmal. Later he tells me, with a touch of pride, that he didn't succumb to the pressure. Getting the better of your rivals is part of our trade.

We squeeze into a car driven by Ajmal's brother, Munir, and return along the same route we took yesterday. The snow is no longer falling so heavily, the sky looks as if it might open up and far away I see the sun peeking over a thick cloud bank. We may well get off the ground: first Kandahar, then Lashkar Gah. I have a telephone appointment with Giovanni Porzio, a colleague who works for the Italian periodical *Panorama*, with whom I have shared other delicate assignments, the last of which was in Somalia. He says he'll join me; he's still in Herat but he's about to get on the road back.

The small plane lifts off at precisely 11:30, Sunday, March 4. It's a two-hour flight. The seats are all full. The plane will stop briefly in Kandahar and then continue to Naranj, in Nimroz province, the extreme southwest of the country. We are flying towards the land of Mullah Omar, the supreme leader, "Amir ul-Momineen," the commander of the faithful. We are heading straight to the front in the Taliban war against the forces of the coalition.

THE JOURNEY

In my readings, Kandahar is always referred to as the city of orange groves. Acres and acres of them spread over an arid plain watered via an irrigation system that was the pride of Afghanistan. The reality is completely different from what I expected. It was the Taliban, as the Pakistani writer-journalist Ahmed Rashid reminds us in his splendid book, who destroyed the orange groves. It may have been out of anger. Or out of negligence. Or it may have been retaliation against the local farmers who opposed the Shariah. During their relentless advance in Afghanistan the Taliban behaved in a similar fashion around Kabul, essentially destroying one of the largest wine-growing areas in the country.

All that remains of the orange groves are a few withered bushes. It's hotter than in Kabul, where, despite the approach of spring, the temperatures are still bracing. The light is strong; the colors are vibrant, yellow and orange dominate. The air is suffocating. There is less dust and less pollution here, but everything around us seems suspended, immobile. American soldiers oversee our arrival.

The terminal is in good shape, almost new, and freshly painted in light blue and white, the national colors. A sign—Kandahar International Airport—bestows a dignified moniker on the edifice. I try to imagine huge jumbos landing on the single runway cut into the desert and unloading droves of passengers still dazed by their long trip. But it's pure fantasy. There's one flight a week, and often it flies straight through to Naranj without stopping. Outside we have to walk down a road full of potholes and rocks to reach Sayed Agha, our driver, who is waiting for us with his brand-new white Toyota Corolla outside the perimeter wall.

I don't know Sayed—Ajmal introduces him as his friend. He is considered the best driver in Helmand Province, a real professional. He comes from a small town near Lashkar Gah and his family is one of the most powerful in the area—a large tribe of influential people, three hundred of them bound by close ties—something that comes in handy if you want to move freely in this land of unwritten but inexorable laws. Furthermore, Sayed is Pashtun, which helps more than a little, for Pashtuns represent the majority here and in Afghanistan as a whole.

Tall, plump, brown haired, lighter skinned than my interpreter, Sayed has a round, open face framed by a closely trimmed black beard. He will open his hazel eyes wide during our rare conversations, which amount to little more than gestures (he speaks no English, and I do not know Pashto). He seems like a good kid, though perhaps a little naïve. His body emits a pleasant odor, giving the impression that he washes frequently, as do the majority of Afghans fortunate enough to have been educated. He attends to every particular of his person with great care, which makes him come off as seeming a little vain: nails clipped, traditional white attire, brown wingtips. Sayed is twenty-eight and already the father of four, with a fifth on the way. Ajmal is a bit envious. He, too, would like a big family but he's decided to postpone fatherhood until he gets back on his feet economically, after having paid for his brother's exile in Belgium and his sumptuous wedding. Sayed is a great believer in good form. He feels responsible for what we are doing and the success of our mission. He moves in fits and starts, rather nervously, but nevertheless manages to transmit calm.

I sit down heavily in the back seat, wrap my head in the turban and follow my two guides' orders: "Never speak, not even at roadblocks when the police ask you questions. We mustn't stick out." Ajmal and Sayed talk and talk, they smile often, they're satisfied, almost excited, about this new job, which promises to increase their standing with the Taliban and open up new contacts among their ranks. I occasionally ask for explanations, trying to get a conversation going. Ajmal translates almost everything with great patience.

In a little more than thirty minutes we're in Kandahar. The Afghan National police and army control the access roads to the city, manning roadblocks with concrete barriers and heavy-gauge machine guns protected by sandbags. The soldiers seem nervous. It's obvious they're on the alert for attacks or ambushes. The city, as opposed to the surrounding districts, is firmly in the hands of Hamid Karzai's government. On the streets the traffic is light; there are many buses that operate as collective taxis, and swarms of motorized rickshaws. Pakistan is close. You can feel it. Quetta, considered the center of Taliban activity over the border, is less than eighty kilometers away. We pull into a parking lot protected by high walls and iron grating that belongs to the Continental Hotel, the only safe hotel in the city, a few steps away from the governor's offices. Ten or so rooms, a common room that doubles as a dining room, two shared bathrooms, the reception run by the owner himself, Amanullah.

There's even Internet access. Ajmal and Sayed spend the whole afternoon together talking in their room. I get online to check the news. There's been an attack in Jalalabad, in the eastern reaches of the country, about six hundred kilometers from Kandahar. There are reports of a firefight that turned into a massacre. American troops are suspected of having reacted excessively, firing indiscriminately into the crowd. Rubbernecks had gathered around the site of the explosion, which injured only one soldier, and maybe some of them threw a few stones, maybe someone pulled out a rifle. In these situations anything can happen—all it takes is one wrong move for all hell to break loose. Though it is not clear what, something went wrong there. The American commanders are avoiding official announcements, trying to buy some time, they're not able to reconstruct the dynamics of the massacre, which, in the meantime, has provoked fresh controversy and protests even on the part of the Afghan police. I call the newspaper and tell them I'm in Kandahar. I suggest we run a piece on these events, which have brought tempers to the boiling point. They're even talking about it in the hotel. Someone points out in stilted English that it's always civilians who end up in the middle. I listen, nod, and avoid comment. I get a call from Radio Capital, a radio station affiliated with *La Repubblica*, and I participate in a brief on-air segment in which I describe what I have seen in Kandahar, the people, the place, and the atmosphere.

Then I call Luisella, my wife. Not a day has passed during our marriage when I have not called her at least twice. She's concerned, but I don't want her to worry. She has never tried to stop me from leaving on an assignment; she's always been supportive, even when her heart was in her throat. I write a piece for the paper and fall asleep immediately, overwhelmed by exhaustion and tension. I wake after about an hour. Fear, an irrational, instinctive fear, assails me. I think of my children, Michele and Alice. When I'm in Rome we speak to each other rarely, but now I want to call them, hear their voices, know what they're doing. During the call, I avoid conveying my anxiety.

I want to distract myself, to placate the anguish that is growing inside me for no apparent reason. My two collaborators are in their room, talking amiably, their bedcovers wrapped around their shoulders, sipping their umpteenth cup of yellow tea sweetened with candies. Their serenity is contagious, and I manage to calm down. "Let's go take a ride around town," says Ajmal. It's dark outside. They maintain that this is best time for a tour: people are out on the streets and there is no danger. It could be interesting but I'm not really up to it, tomorrow we'll be leaving very early, it'd be better to rest now and go to bed early. We eat chicken and rice for dinner and drink tea. Beer, wine, and liquor are against the law. You can find them, occasionally, only in a few places in Kabul. But they're still prohibited substances, symbols of the spiritual and moral decadence of the West.

Monday, March 5. The big day. The day of the interview. Today we leave for Lashkar Gah, sixty kilometers away. The road is in perfect condition, like those I traveled on in and around Kandahar. This particular is not lost on me: here, in the deep south, an area overrun by Taliban, the national government is on top of things, providing infrastructure to the cities and the districts. There is not a single piece of paper or plastic on the ground, everything is clean, tidy, the complete opposite of the chaos that reigns over Kabul. Ajmal tells me that it's all thanks to the new governor, whose predecessor was killed by a car bomb while leaving his office.

We rise early. The hotel is buzzing with activity; everyone, it seems, is already awake. I watch the other guests as we eat breakfast wondering whether or not they know who we are. I'm always afraid that Afghan intelligence is following us. I feel like I'm caught in a vise: I have to hide from the official authorities and protect myself in my meeting with their enemies, the Taliban. Both are skilled and thorough, and I find myself treading a thin, constantly shifting line between the two.

There's no time to go to the bathroom or to smoke a cigarette. Sayed is in his Corolla with the doors open and the motor running. We're leaving. Now. While I'm paying the bill for our hotel, Hamid, the waiter, makes a subtle sign of farewell. Our

eyes meet. He smiles. In the car, I cover my head with my turban, trying to wind it around myself like the Afghans do but
without success. I look foolish, awkward. It takes several
attempts before I get it right. Ajmal and Sayed watch me in the
rearview mirror. They smile, amused by my outfit. But they
actually appreciate my efforts, and they know that the men we
are going to meet will appreciate them, too. Sayed is more talk-
ative today. I attempt to get an idea of the timing of the interview and where it will be held. He has no idea. We'll see when
we get there. The meeting will probably take place in a house;
out in the open it would be too dangerous.

We are racing along a road full of buses, mule-drawn carts,
new cars, and downright wrecks. We're stopped four times at
roadblocks by the Afghan police. They peer hastily into the
cabin to ascertain who we are. I don't move a muscle. The turban around my head hangs down to my shoulders. Only my
eyes are visible. At the fourth and final roadblock we are told
to wait. The police officer looks at me and says something in
Pashto. Ajmal and Sayed reply, telling him that I'm a foreigner.
That's all they say. Before letting us pass, the officer asks if we
can take two other police officers with us. I don't know what
Sayed says by way of an answer, but he refuses and I imagine
he says we're in a hurry and that we're not heading in the same
direction as our two would-be passengers.

Fifty kilometers further on, we turn left on a large sealed
road. Our driver accelerates. He glances in the rearview mirror
and tells me in a few words of English that last night there was
an attack here: a Taliban unit took over a police checkpoint. "It
happens all the time," Ajmal adds. "The police circulate during the day. When night falls they pack up and retreat to the
city." The situation is unstable, says the interpreter. Ten of the
thirteen districts in this province are in the hands of the Taliban. The famous "spring offensive" will begin here and the
games are already underway. The jihadists intend to conquer

the remaining three districts and they rarely pull punches. They attack, they shoot, and they kill. Around here, they prefer open conflict. No suicide bombers. Those kinds of actions are meant for the middle of the country and the north, to spread panic, to lay siege to the central government, to terrorize it. The driver pushes his Corolla up to maximum speed, saying that the road is dangerous, we could be stopped and robbed by bandits. Even during daylight hours, the snares are always waiting. There are no trees, walls, protection. On either side of the ribbon of sealed road, a desert of stone and sand.

I feel vulnerable, easy prey for every kind of thug, militant, or terrorist. I ask how I should behave; I shift positions nervously on the backseat, unable to find a comfortable one, my joints and muscles hurt. Especially my face muscles. They're pulled tight into a grimace that is supposed to be a timid smile. I always do the same thing when I'm nervous: I avoid any outward signs of the tempest raging within me.

We finally arrive in Lashkar Gah and I feel safe. My breathing returns to normal. Sayed knows where he's going. He turns and pulls into a street parallel to the one we were on, then into innumerable small lanes. He traces a wide arc and then stops, with the nose of his Corolla pointed at a brown gate. He sounds his horn several times. A kid about eighteen years old comes to open the gate for us. When we're through it, we stop and get out of the car. We're met by a man. He must be thirty, perhaps a little older. Ajmal introduces him as the director of the Afghan NGO that will host us for the next few hours, time enough for Sayed to meet his contact and to confirm the details of the interview. I prefer that he does it alone. Everything has to go off without a hitch. We're meeting the Taliban, and we don't want anything to irritate or worry them. We must also avoid any word of this making its way to the police. The police must know nothing.

There are roadblocks on the way in and out of the city, yet Lashkar Gah is full of Taliban. Not soldiers or militia, but men who sympathize and who consider themselves Pashtun, real Pashtun anchored to tradition. Ajmal can't stand them. "They're lunatics," he says repeatedly. "They want our country to stay in the middle ages. They're completely out of touch," he insists, barely containing his anger. "They're light years away from Afghanistan. They don't know anything, they're not aware of anything, they're ignorant. To us, education, knowledge, and culture are tools for life and for progress. They want to lock us away in this enormous prison and isolate us from the rest of humanity."

I see more and more turbans, black, white, and dark gray ones. The colors of the Taliabn. As it was in the past, so it is today. I don't see any weapons anywhere, though they are probably hidden somewhere within reach. I spend two hours in the headquarters of the NGO, pacing in and out of the director's room. It serves as his office, but it's also a kind of common room. We drink tea, always accompanied by candies. A woman appears, the first one I've seen in days. She pulls a packet of sweets out of the cupboard and lines the contents up on a tray, which she then offers us. I have cramps in my stomach. I prefer to smoke. I do so outside, out of respect for those who have to put up with a vice that I stubbornly refuse to give up. In the garden around the courtyard there is a man tending to the lawn. He stares at me silently. The woman comes out and signals me to come back inside, they're asking for me. Ajmal and the Afghan volunteer would prefer that I remain inside. We mustn't stick out. My presence might attract too much attention and arouse suspicion.

Later, Ajmal will tell me that even the director of the NGO, an Afghan from Lashkar Gar, avoids leaving his office. He does everything via email, he has collaborators in the region, people from the many villages scattered throughout the districts, who update him on the progress of various projects, all of them financed by the Ministry of Public Health: wells, water filtration, and irrigation systems, the conversion of farms, medicine, campaigns against cholera and tuberculosis.

I will discover a lot of things after the fact like this—apparently insignificant details that are actually essential in order to paint a precise picture of the situation. Many of them will be details that Ajmal kept concealed from me—he would not divulge information acquired from his sources to anyone, me included.

Sayed arrives and tells us that everything's ready—they're waiting for us. I make a call, yet another attempt to reach my friend who works in the hospital run by the NGO Emergency, the only hospital operating in Lashkar Gah. His cell phone is switched off. I'm certain he's in the city, but I'm unable to contact him. I wanted to pay him a visit: he could have helped me understand the situation in this district. He might have told me to be cautious about the interview. I call my colleague from *Panorama*, Giovanni Porzio. He tells me he'll be in tomorrow on a UN flight from Kabul. He says: "I spoke to Gino Strada.[1] He's still in Karthum, Sudan. The only thing he told me was to be careful, the city is swarming with Taliban."

I leave a case containing technical equipment, my trusty knife, the compass I use when sailing, and my torch, at the offices of the NGO. I only take the video camera, my computer, and a notepad. In the pocket of the army-green coat that I'm wearing over my *shalwar* I have three pens.

We turn on to the main road. The traffic is heavy. Right before a bridge we run into a roadblock. Sayed and Ajmal ask me to pull out my press ID card in case the police stop us.

[1] Surgeon, author, and founder of the humanitarian aid organization Emergency. [Trans.]

We'll also need it to identify ourselves to those waiting to meet us for the interview. To the right, fields of opium poppies as far as the eye can see. They skirt the road, even here in the heart of the city. They're blooming. In two weeks the harvest will begin, a ritual that I will soon learn all about from my Taliban tutors. We make it past the roadblock because the police officer is distracted, busy with another car. A hundred meters further on, at an intersection, we turn left.

A boy is waiting for us alongside a gas station. He's the driver's contact, the one who will bring us to the Taliban for our interview. That's how it's been planned, at least I think so. He is completely covered by the shawl Afghans almost always wear. This one is light green. Only his eyes are visible, and I see as he glances towards me that they, too, are light green. His profile is angular, his nose thin and long. He does not return my greeting. He looks straight ahead and points out the road to Sayed. The tension is palpable, as is the anticipation. Nobody speaks, we communicate with gestures, and monosyllabic grunts that might mean everything or nothing.

We drive along a wide gravel road that disappears into the crop fields marked by dozens of deep wheel ruts formed over the years by the passage of thousands of vehicles. We bounce in and out of the ruts in something like a gentle dance, and then turn off onto another, smaller road that cuts across irrigation channels. The water occasionally reaches the doors of the car. We almost get bogged a couple of times. Then, the road ends suddenly. Before us there are only fields of crops. Sayed looks lost. He isn't sure where to go and asks his contact. The boy, evasive, doesn't give him any clear indications. We turn the car around to head back in the direction we came. The maneuver is a little difficult. At the top of a hill, in a circle, we see the shape of three black motorbikes, at least two men on each. I ask if it's them, but nobody answers. We stop the car. The tension is sky-high—this is the crucial moment. I ready myself. Now they'll accompany us somewhere, I think. They'll lead us to the house of the military commander.

The Taliban surround us. A car arrives, another Toyota Corolla. There are a lot of them, at least a dozen or so, and they're all armed. Kalashnikovs, old and new. I look at the gun barrels pointed at us but remain seated in the car, my face hidden behind my *patu*. I wait for orders and instructions. They've already grabbed Ajmal and dragged him out of the car. Now it's Sayed's turn. His contact has vanished. We'll never see him again. Interpreter and driver speak, explain, shout. Their voices are strained. The Taliban pull their hands and arms back and tie them with strips of fabric torn from their turbans. There's talk, lots of it; everyone is talking at once. There is a lot of confusion and I can't understand a thing. Now they grab me and pull me out of the car. They're slightly more gentle with me but decisive in their movements all the same. Their eyes are hard as they look at me. They seem to be asking who I am, what I want, what I'm doing on their turf. I have the impression that they think I'm a spy; their looks are full of suspicion, of hatred mixed with surprise.

I remain immobile as they tie my hands behind my back. Then I begin explaining myself, saying that I'm a journalist. I persist: "We're journalists." I mention the interview with the commander; I say that I'm Italian, and, above all, a journalist. I'm convinced it's all a mistake, perhaps due to something unforeseen. I don't know, maybe a shoot-out that morning with fatalities and injuries among their ranks. Their anger at something of that nature might have changed everything. Yes, I'm sure that's it: a mistake that will be cleared up in no time. I stay calm, fighting back only when they blindfold me so tight it hurts my eyes. I discover I'm claustrophobic. I knew I was, but didn't realize I suffered it to such agonizing extremes. I have to be able to see a little light, even when it's dark. With my eyes closed and covered I can't breathe. I feel like I'm dying, wrapped up in something that's suffocating me.

I react instinctively. I have to free myself of that damned blindfold. I loosen the fabric binding my hands and slip off the blindfold. I protest, repeat again and again that I am a journalist. I'm trying to touch what should be a sensitive point for them by saying that this is not the way to treat a guest, westerner though he may be, one who has chosen to come here to the deep south to give voice and visibility to the Taliban position, to tell the story of a war that the world knows little about.

But these Taliban are soldiers, they obey orders from on high. I protest again; twisting around, I look for other faces and eyes to which I can voice my appeal. Ajmal and Sayed are weeping, emitting feeble laments; perhaps they too feel suffocated by the blindfolds and hoods over their faces.

I'm struck violently on the back, right below my shoulder blade, by the butt of a Kalashnikov. I fall to my knees and raise my hands, I cry, "All right, I'll put the blindfold back on." They hit me again, harder this time, in the head. Everything is spinning, moving in and out of focus, but I remain conscious. Blood seeps into my hair, into my blindfold, which is again tied tight around my eyes. I raise my hands and get shakily to my feet. They tell me to get in the trunk.

I obey. I have no choice. I want them to calm down. In this state, they might well kill me, and I'm paralyzed by the thought of it. I get into the trunk of a Corolla, I don't know if it's theirs or Sayed's. From under the blindfold I see my driver and my interpreter sitting in the backseat of the other sedan. They're immobile, silent. I don't move, huddled in the car trunk as it fills with blood. My heart is beating wildly. My thoughts focus on everything and nothing: my life, the people I hold dear, the newspaper, what is going to happen and what could happen. I'm trying to convince myself that this is all normal. These are the rules, they simply don't trust anyone. I know that the Taliban are hard, violent, extremely distrustful, and I consider the fact that they have blindfolded us normal as well—they are taking us to a place where the commandant is waiting to be interviewed and we cannot be allowed to see roads and houses.

I open the trunk from the inside by pulling a cable my fingers have found. For a second, just for a second, I contemplate trying to escape: I could throw myself from the moving car. But I have no idea where we are and what's around us. It could prove a fatal error. The risk is too high, it'd be better to stay in the trunk. I hold it open a little so I can breathe.

The Corolla stops suddenly. I hear them shouting orders outside. Somebody opens the trunk, which I've just managed to close in time. They prod me with the muzzles of their Kalashnikovs and order me out of the car. I obey. With my hands still tied behind my back I indicate the injury on my head as best I can. I have to stop the bleeding, but with my arms behind my back there's no way to do it alone. I complain, saying this is no way to welcome a guest. They smile, and some of them laugh. They reply as one voice, "journalist, journalist," chanting, mocking. It will be the same story the whole time we are together. On one side, three prisoners taken hostage in what was an unexpected and unimaginable kidnapping, and on the other, fifteen soldiers proud of the prey they have bagged. Kindness and politeness alternate with sudden rage. I believe, I intuit, that they don't want to hurt me. For now. They respect me. I even manage to intimidate them to a certain extent. I obey their orders. I am and will always be a journalist, not a soldier, or a mercenary, and I have nothing to hide, to cover up, or to deny. I can no longer stand the blindfold over my eyes, and ask them to take it off. It is soaked with blood and this complicates matters. Especially for them. They loosen it.

Now I can make them out. They're all wearing gray *shal* -

wars with either black or white turbans. It could be a kind of uniform. I notice a patch on the sleeves of some of their jackets, like military flashes. I read "arba," which in Arabic means four. Perhaps it indicates the unit or brigade to which they belong. They are soldiers, militants, not bandits. This reassures me. Because the idea of being killed here like a dog, without any explanation, reason, or excuse, terrifies me. Everything depends on this gang of boys; I stare at them one by one. Not much older than twenty; armed, hardened, resolute, as strong and thin as nails. Their faces are wide; they treat their black beards with great care, admiring themselves in little hand mirrors they carry in their shirt pockets.

We wait for about an hour with our hands tied behind our backs. The blindfold has fallen down to my neck. I can look around. We are enclosed by the cob walls of something that must be a kind of shelter for livestock. It's old, dilapidated and abandoned. The soldiers push me into a corner, they don't want anyone to see me. I take cover from the sun beside a crumbling wall. At gunpoint I'm ordered back into the sunlight.

Ajmal and Sayed are on their knees, far from me, hands tied behind their backs and white hoods over their heads. They don't complain, and hardly speak. They passively accept this situation. Every so often they say something, mere fragments of sentences, timid protests and desperate attempts to explain. I hear the word "journalist" often, but I have no idea what they're talking about or how our present company responds. There is no discussion, only resignation. We are waiting for someone to arrive, to give a short sharp order that will decide our fate.

The crumbling walls block my view of the surroundings. I take a guess at the time it took to get here, and feel certain that we are not far from where they ambushed us. Perhaps the people who arrested us are merely suspicious—we may still be able to do the interview. In spite of everything, I am optimistic. I try to calm down. I breathe deeply, and even manage to smile. Shaking my head, I tell them in English, "We're here for an interview with a military commander. He knows everything about it and he's waiting for us. If this is your way of protecting your boss, okay. But ask him, at least. He knows, he's been informed, he'll tell you who we are."

The smell of manure is strong. There must be stables nearby, but I don't see nor hear any animals. Even the birds have stopped singing. At the spot where they ambushed us, the birds were raising a racket. Sayed continues his lament but his appeals fall on deaf ears. The Taliban keep us at gunpoint, in silence. I move, slowly. There is a shout, an order, and I move back under the sun, behind a small wall. I can't stay sitting on my heels—I keep losing my balance. I stand up and explain that my back and head hurt, that I'm worried about the blow to the head and the blood that's running down my neck, onto my chest, all the way to the waist of my pants. I have to stop the bleeding I explain, using gestures, smiling in an effort to ease the tension. I'm not dangerous and I have no intention of doing anything other than what they tell me to do. I'm a journalist, I repeat. I'm here for an interview. With a military commander. I look at my companions, asking them to translate for me and to confirm what I'm telling the Taliban. With their heads bent low they mutter something that is muffled by the hoods covering their heads. I look at the faces of the soldiers. One, perhaps the highest-ranking soldier amongst them, smiles. His teeth are brilliant white, the expression on his face almost friendly. He cries: "Journalist, journalist. No, you are a spy! You're a spy, a British spy." He brings his right hand to his neck and drags it across his throat as if it were a knife. Still smiling, he repeats, "Spy, spy, British."

So, they accuse us of being spies, collaborating with the

British forces, who have infiltrators in the Emirate. This accusation can be no coincidence. Of course, it's the standard sentence pronounced by those who arrest you and hold you prisoner; an aggravating factor that will be weighed in the balance when they decide whether you are to live or to die. And it's true that Her Majesty's soldiers have been stationed, together with Canadian soldiers, in southern Afghanistan, in Kandahar and Helmand Provinces, territories that historically have been under Taliban control. So it's natural to assume that spies captured in the area work for MI6, the English secret intelligence services. But to be fingered as one of Her Majesty's subjects so soon after having been captured cannot be due only to the fact that I am blond with blue eyes. There is something unusual about it that arouses my suspicions. So much certainty, almost as if the sentence were already decided. There is no other explanation: someone sold us out. Someone took advantage of the persistent rumors circulating in Kandahar and Helmand Provinces about the arrival of three journalists, one of them a foreigner, and alerted the Taliban to our presence in Lashkar Gah. But who? And why? For money or to curry favor with the Taliban? The only other possibility is that, without our knowing it, we have been used as bait to lure our interlocutors out into the open.

Something must have triggered this reaction on the part of the Taliban. I thought about it over and over again during my captivity. It was something I tried to talk about with Ajmal during our long sleepless nights wrapped in the darkness of our cells, whispering words of concern, reproach, courage, and disappointment as we grew steadily angrier at the absurd situation in which we found ourselves, victims of an unforeseen and unforeseeable abduction. Ajmal would shake his head and apologize: "There has been a misunderstanding," he would say. An error, a misunderstanding. Then, to conclude, with an air of surprise: "I don't understand. The policy of the Taliban has changed all of a sudden. They've never had a problem with journalists. Now they consider us enemies."

Desert Flight

I'm perspiring heavily. Sweat mixed with blood is dripping from my hair onto my face. I try to get a sense of how many and how serious my head injuries are. I can't use my hands, as they're still tied. I ask my captors for help. They look at me in silence and make gestures meant to calm me. They laugh and then become serious all of a sudden. They glance quickly at one another and exchange little guttural noises. Two motorbikes are arriving with four more Taliban on them. Ajmal and Sayed are taken away and thrown back into the Corolla that brought them here. It's not Sayed's car, which has vanished, perhaps hidden somewhere: someone might see it, note the license plate, and alert the police or the Afghan army.

Then they pull me up as well. I cast a final glance in the direction of my two collaborators and tell them in English to stay calm, everything will work out. I'm sure we're heading to our appointment. We'll soon be able to conduct the interview we've been waiting for and put an end to this rather theatrical situation, which, in my opinion, could really have been avoided. I remain composed. The worst is over. For now, they're not going to kill us. The commander must have called, convinced them of their error, and demanded our release. We are the journalists he was expecting.

They put the blindfold back on. I draw in as much air as I can and hold my breath. But I don't protest. I don't want to get hit with a rifle butt again. I obey their orders and they show me respect. This is the first rule we've been able to establish. We all accept it. They push me over to a motorcycle and put a large black plastic bag over my head. The driver of the bike shifts into first. Though my hands are still bound I grab hold of the small rear rack—two pieces of metal. The ride doesn't last long: a few minutes over small hills, a long descent down a dirt track. It is not the same road that Ajmal, Sayed, and I had been on earlier.

I again think of escaping. I imagine the scene: I leap off the bike, then slide, roll, injure myself, free my hands, pull the hood off, and run like mad. I ask myself where I would hide, but above all where I would go, who I could ask for help. It is an impossible endeavor. I would not be capable of such a thing. I'm no soldier. And what's more, I am surprised, confused, but I have nothing to deny, no secrets to protect. I am in the right. Taking flight across this desert would be seen as suspicious, an admission of guilt, the proof that I am indeed a spy. The punishment would be immediate and terrible, perhaps death itself: a blast from a Kalashnikov in the back. The idea alone is enough to paralyze me. Better to stay put, I think, avoid any rash gestures. Better to find a solution to what I still think is a huge, absurd misunderstanding.

A house built out of straw and mud bricks. They send us in one at a time. They take off my black hood and blindfold but leave my hands tied. On the dirt floor there are covers, quilts, and a few cushions. There are fifteen or so people inside, the young men who arrested us and a few new faces, soldiers, dressed in the same uniform. They're young, delicate, and serene, the looks on their faces hard but also possessed, at times, of a certain sweetness. I read curiosity in their eyes. I sense that they still have a few doubts. They believe we're spies, me in particular, but perhaps a slight suspicion that we may be telling the truth has taken hold in their minds.

Our fate is hanging by a thread, subject to an order, a clarification, a decision. Ajmal and Sayed, their heads still hooded, are put in a corner. They speak occasionally. Their voices are calm one minute, hysterical the next. I ask that they be untied, or at least that they be permitted to see. Their faces must be uncovered, I say, as if I were giving the orders. I insist that a degree of dignity and respect for universal rules be maintained. There are unwritten agreements that cannot be violated, those pertaining to basic human rights. I speak and ask that my words be clearly translated into Pashto. For the first time I use the word "prisoners."

They are soldiers, people who are accustomed to orders and discipline, while we are prisoners, but above all journalists. I categorically deny the accusation of being a spy. And my tenacity impresses them. The tension relaxes all of a sudden. My words, translated by Ajmal and perfectly understood by the young soldiers, have had some effect. They look at each other and nod. They take the hoods off my two collaborators and lean their Kalashnikovs and machine guns against a wall in the corner of the room. Finally we manage to converse in a manner that is more relaxed. I talk a mile a minute, more than anyone else. Ajmal has trouble keeping up but he manages to translate my questions and their answers. The Taliban tell me not to worry, they're merely verifying our position. The "investigations" are already underway. There are rules that must be adhered to. They need time. We must be patient. Soon they'll know who we really are.

A door has been left open and, through it, I can see that we are being held in a kind of farm. There are high walls enclosing the building we're in, a garden, a farmyard, a few other structures with adjoining yards. I can also see the owner of all this: an old farmer who walks with difficulty, leaning on a stick. His beard is long and white, his tunic, too, is white. He looks friendly, definitely not part of the group. I smile at him, trying to solicit his support, hoping that he, at least, will believe that I am telling the truth.

The farmer enters our room and leaves a tray with glasses and tea on the floor. He hands out candy and cubes of colored sugar. I greet him in Arabic with the classic phrase, "Salam aleik," peace be with you. I consider it important to show them that I am polite and attentive to good manners. I am polite even when asking if I can smoke a cigarette. They will always allow me to indulge this vice, which for them is forbidden. Maybe because they consider me a kafir, an infidel. Or maybe because they're struck by my courteous ways. Good manners are important, even in extreme situations like this.

The farmer shoots me a serious look. His face is not cruel or evil. He has the air of a wise old man. He leaves the room in silence, without intervening. The young men are talking loudly, joking, asking questions, satisfying their curiosity. They keep us tied up but they allow me to explain some technical features of the devices and equipment they've sequestered. They've taken everything: coat, keys, wallet, papers, pens, notepads, watch, and shoes. They've taken all these things from me almost without my realizing it. I'm practically naked. They've searched my companions, too, and confiscated every last object. The Taliban are fascinated above all by my video camera. It's new, very professional, and very alluring. The one who appears to be the boss pulls it out of its case and turns it on, but cannot go any further: he doesn't know how it works. I stand up with my hands tied, turn my back on them and go over to the video camera. I move awkwardly and it's not easy to keep my balance. Smiling, I make a suggestion: untie me and I'll show you how it works. This is the camera I was planning to use for the interview. They agree. When all is said and done, I represent no real threat. I am their enemy, but not a dangerous one. What's more, I have a beard that is long and white. I deserve respect, I tell them. I am "an old man" and they are young enough to be my children, of which I have two, one twenty, the other twenty-four. *They* have always shown me respect.

When they finally untie my hands, I breathe deeply. I look over at Ajmal and Sayed. The interpreter holds his head low, avoiding my eyes. The driver's eyes, on the other hand, are wide open, he's staring at me, shaking his head as if apologizing. This snag has embittered him, as has the attitude of these people. He must have contacted them dozens of times, and though his previous interactions were by telephone, he wasn't expecting such treatment. When all is said and done, they are Afghans, like him. He is not afraid, but his eyes betray stupor, embarrassment, and shame. He speaks non-stop. I don't know what he is saying; Ajmal doesn't translate. He remains silent. I can only hope to intuit the meaning of the conversation through the facial expressions of my interpreter.

In our two weeks together we will be forced to observe almost absolute silence. I will speak rarely, always careful to avoid even the slightest contradiction. I will only say what is necessary and always in the simplest and most direct terms. I learn to control myself, to know what to say and what not to say, to remain silent and answer only when I am interrogated, to argue and provoke when it is the moment to do so, to ask questions and to listen. Dialogue continues to be important for me. I try to study the situation, identify who exactly was behind our capture, who is giving the orders. It is a strategy that has only one objective: to stay alive, to resist to the very end of the nightmare.

Three hours already. I no longer have my watch but I ask our captors the time and manage to keep track of the passing hours. The soldiers wear identical digital military-style watches on their wrists that are obviously part of the uniform. They were probably bought in bulk, not in Afghanistan, more likely in Pakistan, as they are modern and sophisticated. We drink more tea. With Ajmal's help we talk about anything and everything: religion, family, loved ones.

An older man sticks his head through an opening in one of the walls, a kind of large window. Like the others, he is dressed in military fatigues, his black turban carefully wound around his head and a small cap on top holding it firm. They address him as Commandant. So, this is the man in charge of the group that captured us. Short, plump, skittish, he has a look on his face that is open and curious. They jump to their feet. He vanishes and then reappears through the main door, bending over as he enters. He looks at me, my driver, my interpreter, and then back at me. He studies the injury on my head, the blood that has run down over my face and stained my shirt and pants. He grimaces as he moves nearer. He's concerned and apologizes on behalf of his men, saying it was an unfortunate accident, that this is what happens when one rebels. He says: "You resisted arrest. Our rules and regulations impose a reaction. When one is under arrest, one must obey." After a brief pause, he continues: "In your country don't the police use handcuffs when they arrest someone?" I explain that there's a difference: handcuffs are only used in exceptional cases. Where I'm from, the police must be very careful because the arrestee has certain rights and assurances. I say these words with a smile on my face that is partly genuine and partly redolent of sarcasm and reproach. I tell him, with Ajmal's help, what I have told the others an infinite number of times. "We're here for an interview that we arranged with a military commander." I look at Ajmal. "He knows the name." I press Ajmal. "Right? Tell him what the man's name is?"

Ajmal remains silent. I'm surprised. I can't understand why he's doing this. I feel I can no longer count on him or on Sayed. Perhaps they're too scared. Once more, I try to shed light on the situation. "We're journalists, I'm Italian, you have my passport, you can easily verify that what I'm telling you is the truth. We came here in peace to record the Taliban's position on this war and to ask them about the strategies they intend to employ for the future of Afghanistan." I leave Ajmal enough time to translate.

The commander listens attentively, without interrupting. When Ajmal has finished, I add: "This does not strike me as the most appropriate way to greet people who are professionals, who came to the south to see and to recount what is really happening. You stopped me, arrested me, tied me up and beat me. I was threatened at gunpoint. We came here in peace," I repeat. "Armed only with pens, notepads, and video cameras. Where is the commander whom we were supposed to interview?" The man cuts me off. "He's under arrest," he says. "At this moment, he is sitting in a prison cell in one of our jails. We will deal with him later. He doesn't exist, he's gone, finished."

I have no idea whether this is some banal excuse or the truth—if the latter, it has the potential to bring the world crashing down around me. It's over, I think, we're in it up to our necks. We've been caught in a trap, perhaps one that was laid months ago, planned around a table somewhere. Or maybe it was ordered hastily after someone signaled our presence in exchange for a few dollars. I recall the boy with the green eyes, Sayed's contact: he disappeared during the first frenzied moments of our arrest.

The commander shakes his head, he lifts off my turban and grimaces again—the wound on my head must be serious. He again apologizes and orders his men to get some bandages. I understand from his gestures that my wounds need attention, that I risk developing an infection. He consults with his men and then says: "We arrested you because you entered Taliban territory illegally. We're convinced that you are English spies. You say you're journalists. We must verify some things, and it will take time. If we discover that you are spies we will kill you immediately. If, on the other hand, you really are journalists, we'll ask to exchange you for some of our comrades in prison." I stiffen. I understand now that they have indeed arrested us. I react as a journalist. "But the interview," I ask. "Is it still possible to do the interview? With you, Commander," I suggest. "We could interview you."

I discover that I am no longer afraid. On the contrary, the commander's visit, the chance to speak with a higher-ranking officer, has reassured me. I feel somehow less vulnerable. I am once again a simple reporter who has become the victim of a misunderstanding or a trivial mix-up. Maybe someone tried to be clever and is now paying the price for having overstepped his authority without permission from the local command. I glance reproachfully at my two collaborators and shake my head. I invite Sayed and Ajmal to clarify everything, decisively and definitively, to put a stop once and for all to this mechanism that I still refuse to accept. At first, they reply in monosyllables, then the driver launches into a long and complex discourse. I don't know if what he says is the explanation I requested or an attempt to attenuate the tension that is beginning to mount once more. Ajmal is categorical with me. "They say we're spies. Asking, clarifying, protesting, it's all useless. They always respond in the same way: we're spies."

I wait another hour. The boys come and go. There are always three of them with us. They watch over us but the mood is again relaxed. The sun is setting and the light is weaker now. My arms have been behind my back all this time and they ache. The fabric is cutting into my wrists. They order me to stand up and they put the blindfold back over my eyes. I repeat that I can't breathe with my eyes covered. Three of them lift me up and pull me, my feet dragging, outside. I only have socks on my feet. They laugh and talk amongst themselves, they seem to be discussing my situation with great mirth. They make me walk along a small path between grass and stones. There are puddles of muddy water, patches of wet earth, then sand, earth again, tufts of plants and grass. My heart is beating hard. I'm terrified. I ask where they're taking me. I ask thousands of questions, one after the other. I'm afraid they're going to kill me. A single shot to the back of the head, my body abandoned in a ditch, eyes blindfolded, hands tied. A lifeless bundle without form, dried blood around the bullet hole. I think of Enzo Baldoni, the Italian journalist who was kidnapped and assassinated in cold blood in Iraq before any negotiations could get started.

It's over, I say to myself. I find myself praying. My entire life passes before me as if it were a film. My children, my wife, my mother, the newspaper, the sea, my sailboat, my father, and my siblings. There's no time, I need to see more. The film is running fast, in black and white, the frenzied images pile up. It's over, goodbye to this crazy, unpredictable world that I so desperately love and so violently hate. Goodbye to everyone. My hour has come. I raise my eyes, still blindfolded, to the sky and ask for God's help and His pardon. I ask that He protect my children. I am no longer afraid. I'm ready. Then, suddenly, I feel that they're not going to kill me. I'm certain of it. I don't know why. My instincts tell me so. I want to believe it. Maybe my death is too absurd an eventuality for me to imagine, or perhaps I'm too important for our captors. I'm convinced that they're not going to do it. Not yet, not now. My legs are trembling as we move left. They push my head down and shove me into the trunk of the Corolla. I squirm. I've learned to try to keep my wrists apart when they tie me up so the knots will give a little. But this time the knots are too tight.

The blindfold slips down over my nose and mouth. I can see some light, now, but I can't breathe. I'm going to suffocate to death. I cry out a dozen times, "Please! Please!" I want them to stop, to take the blindfold off me. My breathing is shallower, faster; the blindfold over my nose and mouth begins to grow damp. My mouth and throat are dry. I make a desperate attempt to get hold of a stray piece of fabric with my teeth and pull it off my nose and then my mouth. It is a long, arduous procedure. I try to control my breathing as if I were underwater. I'm convinced I'm going to die. I tell myself that it would be a damned stupid way to die, but I also remind myself that many, many hostages have died like this.

I'm lying on my back, my knees on my chest. I turn over with difficulty and manage to loosen the knots and free my hands. I search for the cable and open the trunk. Fresh air. Finally. Twice, three times, I am tossed from one side of the trunk to the other as the car drives over particularly rough patches. It's torture. I have been taken prisoner by a group of Taliban. I do not know them, nor do I know what their intentions are; I'm alone, left completely to my own devices; I have no contact with the outside world; I am obliged to do everything these young soldiers want me to do, follow orders issued by people far away from here. Death could come at any moment. It is a constant, an obsession that envelops me for fifteen days and fifteen nights with a force, a power that again and again has me gasping for air. I will have to learn to control my panic attacks in order to maintain a modicum of psychological and physical well-being for my increasingly weak and beleaguered body. I calm myself down now, willfully imposing self-control and serenity. I think about yoga, something that will often help me during times of panic over the course of my captivity.

The cable in the trunk snaps. I can no longer even flirt with the idea of escaping. There will be no interview, no meeting. There is no misunderstanding. They have arrested me. I am their prisoner. I even break out laughing, frantic but happy that I'm still not dead. Maybe, I think, we'll make it. We can resist. The country, my country, will not abandon us. My newspaper will sustain us. My friends, colleagues, brothers will help us. I'm certain of this. I have to worry about one thing and one thing only: staying alive.

I'm still shut inside the trunk. I don't move, my head hurts now, my blood is throbbing around my wound. I feel that the blood has clotted, it's no longer gushing out, which is something. But I'm worried: blows like that can provoke internal bleeding.

Half an hour later the Corolla stops. I hear the doors opening, then closing. I understand that they are coming around to open the trunk, that there's going to be some kind of exchange. I hope—yes, for a second I delude myself—I hope that they're going to free us, that the nightmare is over. Pats on the back, more apologies, smiles, maybe a bit of roughing up, but then off we go, freedom awaits. Just one final warning: get out of Taliban territory and never show your faces here again. Naked, stripped bare, robbed of everything, scared, but alive. And free.

But that's not what happens. Though they continue to call it an arrest, this is an abduction. They are convinced they've captured some spies and we remain totally under their control. Or perhaps they already know who we are. They may have identified the newspaper I work for and now they realize they've hit the big time. A big fish caught in their net. Foreign. Italian. Journalist. Excellent merchandise to barter with, to trade for goods, or, even better, for money. The trunk won't open. The cable hangs loose above my head. They go at it in two, then in three. With their hands, their fists, then their guns. I hear one of them snap a clip into his gun. A sharp, metallic, unmistakable sound paralyzes me with fear. I scream that it's broken, that I'm not responsible for it not opening, that they need to use the key. Somehow, I make myself understood. They open the trunk and cool, fresh air gusts in. I can breathe again.

The blindfold over my eyes has fallen down to my neck and I fear they'll be angry, that they will mete out some kind of punishment. Four, five faces smile at me, a confused mass of hands and arms lift me up and out of the trunk. All those mouths repeating in a chorus of shrieking voices: "Please, please, please!" Imitating me, ridiculing me. All I'm thinking about is breathing, I have to get air into my lungs, pull myself together. I tell them my heart is acting strange, that I could kick the bucket here and now, which would be a serious problem for them if their intention is to exchange me for some prisoners.

I look around, turning a full 360 degrees. We're in the middle of nowhere, at the edge of an immense stretch of sand and stones. Before us, to the south, there is nothing but an enormous, infinite desert. The sun has almost set. To our left there's a pickup ready, a Toyota V8 turbo. Powerful, rugged, fast. The flat cargo bed is full of pots, gas cookers, lids, weapons, missile launchers, tanks of water and gas, and a dozen kids with guns at the ready: Kalashnikovs, heavy machine guns, ammunition belts with two hundred rounds a piece. In the cab, together with two fully loaded anti-tank missile launchers are three more Taliban: the commander whom I met in the farmer's house; his lieutenant, a kid with long ruffled hair in a white turban; finally, a third man, older, with a dark gray turban, clearly an officer. He's on a satellite telephone.

A pair of strong arms helps me walk and lifts me into the cargo bed, where I find Ajmal and Sayed. They make room for me. We sit with our back to the passenger cab, leaning up against four large plastic tanks fastened to the cab itself. Sitting like this, our backs will be slightly cushioned when the truck lurches and bounces during our moves.

We huddle in together as best we can, legs crossed, our feet under the pile of covers and mattresses, our hands tied tight behind our backs. Our arms hurt, there is not enough room.

We make do. We're all in the same boat. We feel the same discomfort and the same pain, and we try to put up with it. I will have to get used to the difficulties, the distress, the hunger, thirst, cold, and heat. This is no longer a simple interview. This is the jihad.

The commander, a small plump man whose name I will later learn is Ali, shifts into first and steps on the gas. We're heading south. The pickup takes off like a bat out of hell. The eight cylinders roar, the turbo comes to life with a deafening snarl. The soldiers stare at us, and when the pickup jumps and jolts the barrels of their weapons draw dangerously near our chests. Four soldiers are sitting up front in the cab, their backs to the cargo bed and us; another four are sitting on the side with their legs dangling off the truck. The heavy machine guns are leaning against the steel frame of the cargo bed, barrels pointing outwards, ready for action. In the middle, there are four more Taliban. I can't figure out how they can even fit in—we squeeze together, wriggle for more room, huddle up against one another.

Strangely, I feel almost protected, safe. Now, I fear the others, too: the police, the Afghan army, and the English soldiers stationed in the area. I'm afraid that anyone who finds himself on our tracks might decide to attack. We're hostages, and as such, in addition to being merchandise to be exchanged, we could also serve, if necessary, as excellent shields for our kidnappers. I lower my head. My hands are tied behind my back and there's no way I can reach the edges of the quilt that covers us and pull it up over my chest. The Taliban to my left takes care of it for me. His name is Aleef, one of the few who will tell me his name and with whom I will repeatedly attempt to converse. My wound is throbbing and I feel like I might be running a temperature. Every bump, every jolt, every sudden deceleration makes me feel like my brain is knocking against my cranium. I only hope that nothing serious has happened internally, that there is no risk of hemorrhage. We're in the middle of the desert, there are no doctors around, we don't even have any medical supplies with us.

The getaway is a rally over sand dunes, hillocks, rocks, tufts of grass and wild shrubs. The pickup leaps and lurches and shakes. We complain, cry out in pain, yelp, and curse. The fabric tied around our wrists makes our forearms swell. We are not following any road or trail, we're driving over virgin terrain to avoid encounters that could prove dangerous for everyone. The pickup accelerates. The race is getting faster by the minute. I don't know where we're heading, how long this trip will last, how it will end. But I'm still alive and that is something.

I observe my two companions. Their heads are hanging. Every jolt sends waves of pain through them, too, especially when in the darkness that surrounds us, Commander Ali doesn't see the small sand dunes in our path. When this happens, the pickup stops dead, the front wheels sink into the sand, the rear wheels lift off the ground, and a cloud of dust mixed with small stones and uprooted tufts of grass rises and blusters around us. Then, with a series of leaps and lurches that breaks our backs the truck flies off into the night again. Ajmal is covered in sand. He, like me and Sayed, can do nothing more than shake his head, spit the sand out of his mouth, and cough.

The Taliban soldiers, barely twenty years old, laugh, but it's not cruel laughter; there's no sadism in this contagious gaiety that seems to be part of their very spirit. I haven't seen them, and I will never see them, sad, depressed, or angry. They're a tight-knit group, a crew, and this is their family. They've grown up together. Together, they've studied the Qur'an, which they know by heart in its original Arabic. They live and fight together. Together, they are ready to kill, to cut throats, to massacre. They long to die in battle, together.

They laugh when the pickup struggles over these roller-coaster dips and rises. They want to measure our resistance and make us understand that this is their life. They will share their joys and their sufferings with us, their food and their famine, their thirst and their water. We will never go without. Their attentiveness leaves us dumbfounded, but we will learn to fear it when we discover what they're capable of.

The air is clear, clean, fresh. I look up above me: a black mantle lit by millions of stars shining with a brightness that is only possible in the desert. I'm reminded of night crossings in the sailboat when I was a kid. My father would hand me the rudder, leaving the watch to me. We would be in the middle of the sea, and I, the lone navigator. I would occasionally look at the compass, but I had learned to use the stars to plot my position. I do the same thing now. I can make out the constellations. We're in a different hemisphere but I know which direction we're heading. We're going south, perhaps southwest. I picture the map of Afghanistan, visualize the districts in this part of the country, which I have learned by heart, and realize that the Taliban are taking us as far as possible from the place where we were abducted. We're heading into the southernmost reaches of Helmand province, where they feel safer, where there are no trails and little risk of crossing paths with anyone.

It's past midnight when we arrive in a village surrounded by opium-poppy plantations. It's on the banks of the Helmand River, which here makes one of its many turns before heading west and emptying into Lake Hamun, in Nimroz Province. We'll be staying here for the night. It's pitch black. In the districts we will crisscross over the course of our captivity there is no electricity. When the sun goes down, they light torches, or, at most, a gas-fueled lantern. They go to bed shortly after sunset and wake before dawn.

The Taliban need to find a place to stay. They can count on the people of this village—they have friends here, people who support them. Nonetheless, they avoid showing us around too much. They order me to cover my head and keep my mouth closed. We stop at a widening in the road and a small group of people gathers around the pickup. They're curious. Word has spread. The mujahedeen, legendary heroes cloaked in an aura of mystery, have arrived with their precious booty: three captive spies who were operating in their territory. They are discreet but they cannot help showing us off a little, like game they have just bagged. This is how they reinforce their reputation and increase consensus among the masses.

Men, boys, even young children, draw close. They emerge out of the darkness. Here and there a lighter illuminates their faces as they scrutinize us, silently, their curiosity mixed with condemnation. I'm dying for a cigarette. A man who speaks a few words of English offers me one and I am allowed to smoke it. They let me speak, complain, explain. I talk without interruption to calm my nerves and ease the tension. Almost as if it were a game, a stupid game of soldiers and prisoners. They ask me who I am. I am a journalist, I say. It's a detail, for me a vital one, that I will continue to impress upon the Taliban. The story of three captured spies is an obvious lie, an easy excuse for an arrest that in reality is nothing more than kidnapping, a trap. I obstinately insist on establishing another rule: each of us must assume responsibility for our actions. They must admit that they arrested me, abducted me, that they are moving me to some hideout because they want to use me as ransom. I accept this but demand the respect that any prisoner deserves. I discuss the question with Commander Ali that evening. At first he rejects my demands, but I finally convince him to accept them. He will return to the question often during the seven days we spend together, putting everything in doubt again and again.

It's still Monday, March 5. We move another few kilometers toward an isolated group of houses. The Taliban help us get down from the cargo bed, they unload covers, gas stoves, teapots, weapons, and ammunition. The put us in a barn full of grain sacks, bags of seeds, equipment, old canisters, large containers made of black, smoke-stained clay. We sleep stretched out on a straw mat, all three of us together, our hands still tied with a strip of fabric but mercifully no longer behind our backs. I have certain bodily needs. The tension and the adrenalin mean that I must often ask leave to meet my bodily needs. This will be a feature of my detention. I will also use this need as an excuse to get in some exercise, get a breath of fresh air, try to keep my body in shape, especially my legs, which will end up reduced to something like matchsticks. I use the same excuse to interrupt the monotony of hours and hours stretched out on makeshift beds and to calm the waves of panic that assail me, at times so violently that I can't breathe. That night, Commander Ali warns me: "Once you're inside your cell, you don't come back out. If you knock for your needs, we'll kill you."

We sleep like logs. Tired, distraught, incapable of fully accepting a situation that we continue to think of as a bad dream, a nightmare from which we expect to wake sooner or later and recount to our loved ones as if it were a sign to be interpreted. But that's not how things turn out.

The sudden wake up call—the small steel door opening and slamming against the wall—brings us hurtling back to reality. The Taliban on guard emits a short, sharp order: time for morning prayers, the first of five such prayer sessions that every Muslim must observe daily. This one is among the most important; the prayer must be recited according to a precise ritual and followed by a series of gestures. You must wash your hands, feet, face, ears, nose, mouth, arms, and elbows first. A method for eliminating all the impurities absorbed by the body during the previous day and night. You can skip these ablutions only if you have not yet taken care of your own needs. It is a delicate and very spiritual moment in which one comes before God. It is a question of respect and devotion.

I do not pray to my God that morning. They hand me a small empty canteen, one of those used to hold oil for cooking, and jerk their heads toward a spot where I can go to empty my bowls. I will not be out of their sight, and more importantly, the spot lies away from Mecca, the direction in which the militants, Sayed and Ajmal, are all praying. I watch them from afar, sitting on their heels. Mine have grown sore, unaccustomed as I am to this position. They insisted that I sit this way right from the start, and not, as they repeat with disdain, "western style." I will grow so used to this position that even two days after my liberation I will not be able to assume others without pain.

They pray as a group, one beside the other, including my two collaborators, whose hands have been freed for the occasion. Each man kneels on his own carefully laid mat, and calmly performs the same gestures to a rhythm set down by a boy who, because of his seniority, his religious knowledge and acquired merit, officiates over the rite, alone, in front of the group.

Tuesday, March 6. The pickup is ready. The cargo bed is full of covers. The weapons are already in place. Ten minutes after having been woken, time enough to gulp down some tea and a few pieces of bread, and we're on our way. They tell me to get down, remain wrapped in my shawl, hidden under the dirty, dusty covers. I vanish beneath that mountain of wool, plastic and cotton and immediately begin to have trouble breathing. There's no air. With my hands, which, fortunately, are tied in front of my body today and not behind my back, I open a small spy hole through which a little air and light enter. I have been told we have to cross a river on a small barge and that nobody, including the ferryman, must see me. So I obey their orders and stay hidden beneath the covers.

Ajmal and Sayed, on the other hand, don't need to hide. Only their hands, tied with a length of fabric, are hidden beneath the covers. They're Afghans. They can be swapped for Taliban soldiers currently in jail. Our captors watch them like hawks. If they make some sign, try to send some kind of signal, even the smallest, with their eyes, we may be killed on the spot. It'd be a trifling thing for the mujahedeen and nobody, certainly not the inhabitants of the village, would dare to say a thing.

Hidden under the mountain of covers I hear the Toyota maneuvering onto a barge. The motor of the little iron ferry starts, accelerates, chugs, and we begin the river crossing, twisting and rocking in the strong current. I pray to God that we make it to the other side. With my hands tied I'd never manage to swim to safety if we end up in the water. But after a few minutes we reach the shore.

The pickup roars to life again, and starts back on its mad race. To the south, further and further south, towards a second and then a third stretch of desert. The sky is blue, the sun has risen on my left. The Taliban push aside the covers and tell me that I can come out, thanking me for having remained hidden and quiet. One at a time, they pull out a small round silver container with engravings on the lid, and figures and symbols in Pashto. Each is full of a green powder. They arrange a line of the powder on the palms of their hands and then lick it up with their tongues. It is something they repeat every couple of hours.

I imagine it's some kind of drug. When I ask them about it, the boys laugh and offer me some to try. It doesn't strike me as such a good idea. Ajmal explains that it is a kind of hallucinogenic tobacco; you put it in your mouth and wait for your natural laboratory to call forth its effect. He also tells me it's a very strong stimulant. "They're used to it," he warns me. "If you use it, the effects might not be so good." I ask, needling them slightly, whether their religion allows such a thing, given that they don't drink, don't listen to music, don't engage in sex, have never read anything except the Qur'an, and distrust anything that smacks of the depraved and impure west. They explain that there are no prohibitions concerning drugs, and that it's not even a drug, really.

Aleef, the Taliban with whom I exchange a few words of English every so often, replies, needling me and provoking me in return: "You smoke cigarettes, we eat tobacco." I suggest he smoke a cigarette, that he try something new. He tells me it's impossible. It isn't the Qur'an that forbids smoking but the commander in chief, Mullah Omar, "Amir ul-Momineen." He says this seriously, without the hint of a smile, which would be seen as showing a lack of respect for the supreme leader. He explains that Omar issued a special fatwa after consulting with the other ten members of the Supreme Shura. In that moment, whoever had been a smoker was no longer a smoker.

Indeed, in the fifteen days we spent together, I never saw one of them with a cigarette in his mouth.

The pickup flies over the desert dunes. We tear along old tracks hidden by the shifting sands and dotted with small sharp rocks of various colors: yellow, purple, light blue, black. We drive over countless small hills stretching all the way to the horizon. After a couple of hours we see the outline of two mountains rising up out of an immense plain populated only by herds of camels and mules, and flocks of small black and brown lambs with thick wool. Many are wild, but when I look more carefully I can make out the shape of a small boy shepherding others with a stick. We are hundreds of kilometers from the nearest town. Yet there he is, alone, perhaps with nothing more than a flask of water, accustomed to wandering for days and days in the middle of this desolate land.

The landscape is devastatingly beautiful. Dunes rise out of the desert floor like ocean waves during a storm, their crests sculpted by the wind. As far as the eye can see, a succession of rolling hills, marshes, small lakes, and palm trees. A tiny black dot interrupts the horizon. It is moving away from us, trailed by a cloud of dust. One of the Taliban kneels, stares long and hard at the horizon, looks around, and then turns back to that suspicious presence. He yells something, the others reply and pick up their weapons. They pull him down and shake him up a little. One at a time, they, too, straighten up and stare at the black dot for a while.

I look at Aleef and ask him, worried: "Americans? Americans?" He shakes his head and says there's nothing to worry about. He glances in the direction of the suspicious dot one more time, and then begins to sing at the top of his voice. A song I will hear often during our days of captivity. Our warders themselves will shout it, it will play on the Taliban's car stereos; soldiers will pass around a cassette with the same song on it. There is no musical accompaniment, only sweet words, sung by young voices that are almost feminine. No fanfare, but rhythmic slogans, battle songs. A repetitive dirge burgeoning with melancholy. These songs are the hymns of the Qur'anic student movement. They tell stories of battles, conflicts, but also of a better world, a world that is more just, in which everybody lives safely and in peace, purged of thieves, hypocrites, and murderers. But also without women, progress, culture, books, music, dancing, cinema, and television. A world anchored to the past, to the age of Mohammed Himself. A great calm oasis without history, without emotions, and without feelings, founded on the doctrines of the Qur'an, the book that Allah bequeathed to the earth and in doing so eclipsed the other two volumes belonging to the great monotheistic religions.

I will speak often about the future Islamic utopia with these young men, who, however young, are conscious that their deaths await them around the next bend in the road. They remind me of a pack of wild dogs: strong, tight, mad, ferocious, curious, cunning, decisive. But above all, happy, convinced that they are in the right, ready to sacrifice themselves, to martyr themselves so that they may attain truth, make the great leap to paradise, the only real goal of an existence that is disfigured, limited, and totally closed to the world.

The mountains that I saw on the horizon a while back now form a range marking the end of the desert. We slow down and travel along trails that have been cut into the mountains by the motorbikes and pickups of drug and arms smugglers. Ajmal explains that this is a border zone. He thinks he recognizes some features, but he's not sure. We must be close to the Pakistan border. The mountains close around us, we are in a narrow gorge that finally opens onto a plain punctuated by large rocks and brushwood.

Commander Ali told us that he was taking us to the Movement's most important hideout, the "main base." But he lied. There is no base camp. In time I will learn how deceitful the religious students are. They will tell us a mountain of lies. And somehow I don't believe they do so just to keep us in the dark: my sense is that it's part of their nature.

At the bottom of this valley protected by high peaks there are two buildings made of mud and straw. They are enclosed by a perimeter wall with two entrances, one to the east, and one to the west. Perhaps these buildings are habitually used by the Taliban, though there are no traces of a training camp or anything else of that nature. The militants need to hide, particularly from spying eyes overhead. During the night especially, but also by day, I hear the rumble of spy planes. This incessant surveillance agitates our captors and explains why they make us move hideouts a total of fifteen times in two weeks, sometimes twice a day.

Right now, this sound reassures me. It makes me feel that I have not been abandoned, that finally, after a long silence, the alarm has been raised. But it's only conjecture. There's nothing that really confirms my hypothesis. I am inside a bubble, and here only the desert silence is audible. The remote surveillance of these zones is standard procedure. Using drones, the English, with the help of the Americans, observe and record every movement on every inch of ground in this part of the country. We are perfectly visible. We stay inside all afternoon. The floor of these rectangular edifices is made of earth: there are four holes for windows and an entrance without a door.

The tension has eased. Now begins a kind of interrogation that will last nearly a week. No torture, not for now. The Taliban will take turns talking to each of us, one at a time, asking us who we are, what kind of life we lead, what we think of Afghanistan, of the war. What are our ideals, our projects, our dreams? It is not mere curiosity but part of the "investigation" ordered by the leaders of the group. Every dialogue will be dominated by a recurring theme: religion.

Commander Ali is sitting in front of us. He turns first to me, the foreign journalist. They are more curious about me than about the others. He begins to talk to me about Islam. He apologizes repeatedly for the head injury that his men inflicted on me and explains that things like that don't happen often, that their prisoners are not usually treated in that way. References to Guantánamo, to the military base in Bagram, are frequent: "They are not inclined to show prisoners the same attention there. Our brothers are tortured." He encourages us to consider ourselves guests rather than detainees. It doesn't take much—a quick glance in the direction of the Kalashnikovs pointed at us, or at the miserable state in which we find our-selves—to glean the truth. But he insists, he orders his men to free our hands and begins firing questions at us.

I don't hide anything from him. I tell him that I was born in Karachi, in Pakistan, that I even have a Muslim second name, Amir, like that of Mullah Omar, their supreme guide. They will never use this name in my presence. I will always be Daniele to them, for the name Amir represents a sacred title, one that Mullah Omar gave himself in 1996 at the Mosque of the Sacred Cloak in Kandahar, not far from the Mausoleum named after the nation's founder, Ahmad Shah Durrani. The Mullah made a gesture of great symbolic importance that year. To legitimize his role as leader, a charge he had received from God himself, he removed the cloak of Mohammed from where it was housed and exhibited it before a teeming crowd of Taliban.

Flogging in the Name of Allah

I repeat the name Amir, slightly mangling the pronunciation. Commandant Ali does not correct me. He makes no reference to the great spiritual leader. So I do: "The Mullah Omar!" I merely want to show him that I know whereof I speak, that I know about his past, the legends associated with him, and his flight by motorcycle during the coalition's military offensive in 2001. Though the last detail made many westerners grin at the time, it was considered normal around here—the motorcycle is still the most common means of transport used by the Taliban.

Ali unwinds his black turban. His hair is short, almost shaven, and quite a contrast to his long, black, wiry beard, which he strokes whenever he gets nervous. It appears I have pressed one of his buttons; he is visibly flustered, he strokes his beard. There won't be any more direct references to Mullah Omar. Only once, near the end of our captivity, on the eve of my release, Mullah Dadullah, the man we were supposed to interview from the start and the true architect of our abduction, will speak of "Amir ul-Momineen," the Commander of the Faithful.

Ali returns to the subject of Islam and explains that I have a decision to make. The fact that, in theory at least, I am half Muslim and half agnostic should facilitate my conversion. All the preconditions exist for me to become a good Muslim. As he is telling me this, his excitement mounts; his large, open face glows in the setting sun's red rays.

Ajmal sits down beside me. Sayed keeps his distance, listening but not participating in the conversation. I imagine he's thinking about what has happened to us, maybe deciding what to do.

I am prudent in replying to the commander. It's a choice that should be pondered at length, I say, perhaps after studying the Koran and reading other books on Islam. I have read many, but not enough to consider myself an expert. "It would be frivolous," I object. Ali agrees, but he becomes more and more fervent. Two other Taliban draw near. They calmly sit cross-legged on the straw mat that also serves as a mattress and join in the conversation. Ajmal seems relaxed. In addition to translating questions and answers he provides insight into the strategies adopted by our captors. Trust and mistrust will be constant companions for the entire length of our captivity; bitter disappointment will alternate with moments of unexpected hope. I will learn how to weigh every move, every gesture, and how to ascertain the hidden meanings of details that could otherwise be misleading.

The Taliban are well trained in interrogation techniques; they are adept at administering the right doses of kindness and aloofness, affability and violence. They are skilled, very skilled. But they are also very sensitive to religious questions. Their enthusiasm for conversations about God and the divine laws that determine our lives and form our souls is not always a calculated means to an end. These young men live for Allah; they consider him the center of their very existence.

Ali does not loosen his grip. He is tenacious. I smile, trying to make things difficult for him, and ask whether he thinks it is right that my conversion should happen at this precise moment, in this place far removed from the world, and above all that it should happen while I am in captivity. He's fired up. He is convinced that my willingness to discuss the matter is the first sign that I may eventually yield, and moving closer, he persists. "For him," Ajmal explains, his expression dubious and his voice flat and emotionless, "it would represent an enormous success. He says it would bring him honor. His bosses, the *helder*, the ones that want to see us, would be willing to let us go, maybe. It would be a fitting price to pay for our freedom." I have a sudden inspiration. "Commander, would you let me go if I became a Muslim?" Ali nods several times, and adds, "However, if you're sure of this decision, you must take the first step, an essential one for us Muslims." "What step is that?" I ask, curious. Ali skirts around the subject, he's a little embarrassed. He asks Ajmal to inquire as to whether I am circumcised. I answer no, I am not circumcised. The commander is disappointed but indicates that there is no real problem: the matter can be resolved. He says it is, however, an indispensable step in my conversion.

I believe he's still testing my courage. He's been laying a trap into which I have not fallen, I tell myself with a touch of pride. He wants to find out just how rooted my religious sentiments are. Freedom in exchange for circumcision. My demeanor is serious. "It can be done," I conclude. "But I doubt your bosses, the *helder*, will agree." Ali jumps to his feet. "I'll call them immediately, let's see what they say. In the meantime, I'll look for a doctor. It's a simple matter, clean and precise." I shake my head, terrorized by the idea of being circumcised in a sheepfold, amidst fleas and mice, with an old rusty knife. I dampen his enthusiasm immediately: "If I must make this decision, I want to make it as a free man. Otherwise it would be a flippant and hypocritical act. In the Koran," I continue, "the Prophet unconditionally condemns hypocrisy."

The conversation moves on to other topics, from everyday life to politics. Ali dwells on the American bombings, which, he repeats often, "mainly kill defenseless civilians, women, and children." I am in no condition to respond. Then he goes back to religion: only Muslims can hope to enter Paradise; the rest of the world, which lives in ignorance, is condemned to heresy and perdition, to nothingness after death. His is a desperate appeal to the great religious communities of the world to convert before it is too late, before the darkness of the apocalypse descends and the hour of the final audience with God strikes.

Before the sun disappears in the west prayers are said. I pray to my God as well, my hands joined, my gaze fixed before me, crouched in my corner, my anguish growing.

I fall asleep. A little later on, I wake with a start and lay staring at the ceiling. I realize for the thousandth time that this is not a bad dream. I'm not at home; I'm not in a hotel; I'm not in Kabul. I'm a prisoner of those same Taliban whom I wanted to interview. No matter how things turn out, my newspaper has its story, and somehow this fact consoles me. My reporter's instincts have prevailed, and those same instincts are my best weapon of defense. Against myself and against my captors.

They wake us up during the night, a few hours before dawn on Wednesday, March 7. There are strange noises outside, agitated voices. I shake Ajmal and ask him if he can tell what's happening and if there's some kind of problem. Closed, by now, behind that tormented gaze of his, those eyes staring into space, virtually dumbstruck, he says he doesn't have any idea. He too has heard the commotion. "Maybe," he says, "they're going to move us." He's right. He hears one of the child soldiers marshalling the others. The ochre-colored Toyota with blue and yellow panel stripes along its sides and Dubai plates is ready. We climb into the cargo bed. Our hands are tied in front of us, thank God. Our tortured faces and protests during the earlier moves must have had some effect on our kidnappers.

We drive for about ten kilometers, at a crawl, following tire tracks left by those who have traveled this same route before us. We enter a gorge and the truck stops at the top of a cliff, where it can be easily and well hidden behind rocks and bushes.

The cargo bed is reserved for us three. It is full of covers and blankets. We fall unconscious in no time. Meanwhile, the Taliban sort out guard duty, and those whose turn it is to watch over us take up positions on the outcrops surrounding our improvised jail, each brandishing a weapon. The others wrap their covers around themselves. They sleep hugging their rifles, with one eye open, like sphinxes.

My hands are still tied. I twist and turn nervously, unable to find a comfortable position. My whole body aches, though surprisingly I have no internal pain, and even my stomach, which has been ruined by ulcers and gastritis, seems to be holding up. We've been drinking well-water for two days, we warm ourselves with cups of yellow tea, and we eat potatoes; every now and again we tear flesh from the small bones of an animal they pass off as chicken. More likely they are wild birds caught wherever we stop. I'm afraid I'll contract some kind of viral infection, but apparently the adrenalin produced by the constant tension has reinforced my immune system: over the entire fifteen days I will not have a single disturbance.

I sleep for a few hours. When I open my eyes, the sky is pale blue. Little by little, the dawn light sketches the outline of the mountain peaks hanging over us. There's a fire crackling a few meters away from the pickup truck, and the smell of burning wood wafts in our direction. Those Taliban who were not working the dawn shift wake one by one. Silently they pick up their water canteens and go looking for a secluded spot. Everyone moves mechanically—there is no more need of orders. Orders were given mostly for our benefit, but by now we know the rhythms, the rituals, what has to be done and when. I wrap myself in my shawl, the *patu* that I use as pillow, turban, tablecloth, and head covering, and with my hands still tied in front of me, I crouch down near the fire. I make sure to greet them, as I will do throughout. According to the reply I receive, I will know what to expect from the day.

The commander is avoiding me. The idea of my converting to Islam in exchange for our freedom appears to have come to nothing. I'm still waiting for an answer and, in theory, if he has spoken to his bosses as he purportedly intended to, I have one coming to me. The problem is the spy planes that are forever flying overhead. The Taliban are worried and distracted.

We keep moving south, into and out of gorges, over plains— the landscape is all the same. A brief stop, stretched out in the sand, in a tiny deserted village of mud and straw; time enough to draw water from a well and fill the water tanks, and then off again, slowly, watching the roads carefully, scanning the mountaintops, alert to the sound of the occasional motorcycle or car heading in the opposite direction. We never meet anyone on the road—anyone who drives a pickup here knows the area well enough to avoid the main route and opts for hidden trails that run parallel to ours.

We leave the pickup behind and continue on foot. They untie our hands because we have to climb a hill and we need our arms and hands. They keep us at gunpoint, but they know that we won't try to run. For now. They're especially worried about me. They consider me a rebel, a hothead, capable of some impulsive act. I have the impression they are following precise orders, and if one of us were to escape, they would not hesitate to kill him.

Two buildings in ruins appear at the top of the hill. Two adjoining rooms, the roof partially caved in, and a kind of small sunken pen full of rubbish, the remnants of others who have passed through here before us: paper, plastic, pieces of cloth, an old sweater, fabric that would have once been part of turbans, shirts, and pants. With a stick, the one whom I have heard called Hassan, the oldest Taliban (he is probably about thirty years old, with a thin beard on a lean, hard face), pushes this graveyard of humanity in all its variety into a corner of our prison cell. He picks up an old straw mat worn to a thread and full of dust, spreads it on the stony dirt floor and barks, "Sit over there." He points to the opposite side of the room where there are two openings in the wall that serve as windows, as far as possible from the entrance, which is low, tight as a small tunnel, and without a door.

I crawl into a corner of this hole and try to pluck up my courage. I keep my mind busy by forcing myself to focus on details, colors, sounds, the days of the week. But thoughts continue to bluster through my mind—like hurricanes, they shake me to the core and overwhelm me. I will suffer from frequent headaches. My head will feel full to the point where, more than once, I will feel that it is ready to explode. I don't speak much, I lose myself in other worlds, other issues, and I almost always fall asleep sitting up. I usually do not remember my dreams. But since I've been in captivity, I recall them vividly. Dreams about all manner of things. My mother, my father, who died last summer, my wife, my children, the newspaper, my colleagues. They are not nightmares, but the situations are absurd, improbable. I feel like someone on the outside wants to talk to me, to transmit messages and thoughts. A kind of telepathy that travels thousands of kilometers to reach me in this forsaken place. It comforts me to think this might be true.

For thirty-six hours we remain where we are, almost comatose. I run through the days that mark off our captivity. It's March 8. Aleef, the soldier who, to a certain degree, has become my reference point within the group, charges into the cell and asks Sayed to leave. He obeys and follows the Taliban out. Ajmal is still sleeping, or perhaps he is awake, but he keeps his eyes closed. I'm not worried about our friend; there has been no cause for tension, nothing of any particular relevance has occurred. Almost an hour passes and Sayed does not come back. Now I am concerned. I don't know where he is, I have not heard a single cry, a single sound, not even the usual low murmur that reaches us from beyond our cell. I'm starting to think that they've gone, all of them, that they've let us go. Alone in the middle of the desert, but free.

It's only an illusion. Sayed appears at the door; he bows his head and crawls into the hole that serves as our prison. His face is white, his eyes miserable slits; the corners of his mouth are lined. He shakes his head. He is crying. Then he curses through clenched teeth: "Fuck Taliban, fuck Taliban!" I want to know what happened, and I ask Ajmal to translate. The interpreter has just woken up, his face is heavy, drowsy, but he, too, is shaken by the sight. Sayed says that he was beaten on the back and the legs, and then tells us exactly what it was that finally made him panic: they tried to strangle him. He mimes the movements: hands grabbing at him from behind, then something like a length of cord around his neck, tightening so that he could not breathe. They stopped only when his eyes began bulging out of their sockets and he collapsed. He thinks he passed out for a few seconds. He's afraid. So are we. I look at Ajmal, he looks at me, and we put mute questions to one another, enveloped in a weighty silence.

It is my interpreter's turn. They take him from our cell and lead him away. Sayed mutters something in English—he asks me not to betray him. If I am interrogated, he implores, I must say that I gave him fifty dollars a day to be my driver. Ajmal warned me of this last night: if they interrogated him, he would say the same thing. You gave me two hundred dollars, he said, for the whole five-day journey to the south. This aspect had not occurred to me. Apparently Sayed and Ajmal had already dealt with the question in their conversations with the Taliban, but nobody told me.

We're in the middle of the investigation now, and they want

to know who the five thousand dollars belongs to. It's actually Ajmal's fee, paid in advance, for setting up the interview. I was stunned by his request at the time, for the price struck me as unusually high. We discussed the matter in Kabul, and his response to my objections was firm: "All the TV stations pay the same amount. It's also a kind of safeguard." I explained that I work for a newspaper and wouldn't be needing the kind of support that entails an entire crew. But I intended to use a video camera, and this fact alone put me in the same category as his previous clients. I'd been about to give up on the interview. Ajmal had become too costly. But in the end, slightly annoyed, I accepted.

It was right before they stopped us. We were traveling along that final stretch of road, a road littered with large stones, and I handed him the money. Four thousand dollars—in the end, he had given me a discount. He put the money in his pocket and that's when they stopped us. They found the money straight away. The Taliban suspect that the money is mine, but, on the other hand, it could just as easily be the fruit of Ajmal and Sayed's labors, as spies. They want answers: they don't remember whose jacket they pulled the money out of when they searched us.

I reassure Sayed. I tell him there's no problem: what he said during his interrogation seems credible to me. It's only logical that that wad of cash, the four thousand dollars, belongs to me. But I'm underestimating the shrewdness of the Taliban, together with their desire to squeeze me and, as they will continue to do, punish me for every lie, even the smallest.

It's my turn. Ajmal is sitting on his heels in front of the door to the second room. He looks down, without a word. His face is dry. He has not shed a tear. They take me into the first room. They're all standing there in a circle. They tie my hands and my arms behind my back with some rags and move me to the center of the room. I ask if Ajmal can be present. I know that I'm going to be interrogated, and at this point there can be no misunderstandings: Ajmal must be in the room to translate their questions and my answers.

They begin by asking what I had in my computer bag. I list off some items: books, pens, notepads, a red notebook, receipts, and money. How much? I don't know, perhaps two, maybe three thousand dollars. It's the truth. I watch them, waiting for a reply that does not come. They ask once again: What did I have in my computer bag? I picture my black computer bag, mentally searching the inside and outside pockets. Maybe I've forgotten something. But I have no reason to hide anything. Wires, technical equipment, network cables, I say. "I don't know what else to tell you, really. That's it. You have it now, you can check."

What item has betrayed and condemned me, I wonder. Nothing comes to mind, unless they saw some news article they didn't like. Though that seems unlikely—they're all in Italian. There are numerous dispatches from Jerusalem: maybe they object to my trips to Israel. But many Palestinians still live in the Holy City. I promptly dismiss these possibilities. That they object to something they found on my computer seems suddenly too complex a hypothesis. These mujahedeen would not be able to translate articles written in Italian. What's more, they've never even seen a computer before. Indeed, the Taliban who are interrogating me focus on the money, they want to nail the driver, maybe the interpreter, too. They use me as a witness for the prosecution. They're fishing for something that will confirm their suspicions. They know that the four thousand dollars is mine, but the important thing is to figure out who I paid, my driver or my interpreter. Whoever it was, they hold him responsible for having introduced a spy into their territory.

They ask me how much the interpreter and the driver cost,

all together. I reply according to the agreement I have with my cellmates. I don't betray them—our versions are identical. My interrogator's name is Munir—the one who travelled in the cab of the pickup and who wears a white turban. He orders me to kneel and then to lie down on the floor. I'm waiting for my punishment, my arms stiff behind my back. I remember what Sayed told me, that they had tried to strangle him. Out of the corner of my eye I can see a Taliban at my shoulder, moving closer. It looks like Hassan, the oldest among them.

He has a length of wire in his hand that he shapes into a noose, twisting the two ends together. He draws closer. I prepare to hold my breath; they're going to tighten the wire around my neck so that I can no longer breathe. But that's not what happens. At the cry of "Allah Akbar" two, three, four, I stop counting at twelve, hard blows fall from on high. My back arches, I try to soften the blows by tightening my back muscles. But those men standing over me lash out with wild fury. They don't stop for a second. They beat me on the back, on my thighs. The whistling as the lengths of rubber garden hose that they use to flog me is overpowered by their cries. They flog me and shout. Tears line my face, which is covered in dirt and dust. Finally, I yell, "*Basta, Basta!*" It comes out like an order, but it is a supplication. *Basta*, enough, is a word they use in Pashto as well.

The one holding the wire tight in his hand moves in front of me. I recognize him—it's Hassan, all right. He orders them to stop, and the soldiers obey. Some of them laugh; others lift me to my feet. Munir, the boy with the white turban, comes over to me and says they're just following the rules, they're Taliban, nothing personal. I feel insulted and humiliated, but I object weakly: you don't beat civilian prisoners. I remind them that I am an old man, and above all a journalist, a figure that is considered neutral in any armed conflict.

"Why don't you take soldiers prisoner?" I ask angrily, the

pitch of my voice getting higher, and my tone becoming dangerously fervent. "Why take a journalist prisoner, someone who came here among you just to do an interview, unprotected, without any weapons, armed with only a pen and a notebook?"

I'm up on my feet now. My clothes are filthy with dirt and dust, and I'm screaming at Ajmal, who has not moved, who appears paralyzed, to translate word for word. He must not change anything. He must not leave out the adjectives or alter the intonation. I can't tell if he does what I say or not. I believe he does not, in order to protect us and to avoid further violence. He mutters something, his voice meek.

I'm beside myself. The situation is becoming unbearable and my resistance has reached its limit. I turn around without waiting for their replies and head toward the prison-cell hole that awaits me, walking a little like a duck because of the pain, my hands still tied behind my back. I prepare myself to face a long and difficult time in captivity—I am a prisoner, nothing more. That other Daniele, the journalist, foreign correspondent for *La Repubblica*, is still back in Lashkar Gah. Munir, the Taliban who was in charge of the interrogation, comes over to me. I turn quickly and stare darkly at him. He smiles as he says: "So, we managed to squeeze a few tears out of you. You never cry."

He's right, I think. I only cry in moments of deep sadness and desperation. I will cry more than once over the course of these fifteen days, mostly at night, alone in the middle of the desert—brief silent fits of sobbing full of anger and fear.

Munir unloosens the knots around my wrists, grabs my left hand and discovers that I'm still wearing my wedding band. He tries to pull it off, but I make a fist. "No," I say. "No." With a bemused smile he opens my hand and, as he stares into my eyes, he slips the ring off my finger. He studies it, turns it over, looks back at me, and drops the ring into his pocket. He raises his index finger. It's a threat, his way of reaffirming the same idea he will repeat many times over the next weeks: I'm in charge here.

I whisper an insult that he duly ignores.

I return to the dark, cold, damp pen that is my jail cell. Ajmal is still being held outside. I find Sayed folded in on himself, huddled in a corner of the room. He looks at me with his large eyes wide open and mimes being flogged. He's looking for confirmation, he wants to know what they did to me. He then mimes strangulation, shakes his head, and weeps. Again he whispers: "Taliban, fuck you, fuck you!"

He has looked death in the face. He says these men want to kill us. I understand his feelings: we have been deceived and we're starting to distrust everything and everyone. We can never let down our guard, we must always attempt to see what is hidden behind acts that seem conciliatory; we have to foresee every danger and correctly interpret sudden mood changes. We must study our captors more carefully. These Taliban are cunning, adept at discerning a prisoner's psychological state. They are no longer young madrassa students—they're soldiers. I tell the driver that they beat on my back and legs. They didn't try to choke me as they did him.

Ajmal returns to the cell. They haven't tortured him further; Munir and the others kept him back only so that he could translate my last words, which they hadn't understood. He explains that he, too, was flogged on his legs and thighs. But he doesn't complain. Sayed is the most frightened among us. I have the impression that they said something awful to him, some kind of terrible threat. He is turning over the implications of some change in the situation that apparently concerns him alone. They still consider him a spy, the only real spy in our little group.

They bring us something to eat. It's midday but we're not hungry. We hurt all over. We're humiliated and depressed. I dwell upon this violence and torture for some time. The thought that this might happen had never really occurred to me, but faced with what just took place I must resign myself to the possibility of further days of mental and physical anguish. Once again, I pray. I ask my God to spare me further interrogations. I am willing to remain a prisoner for many days yet, but the idea of having to suffer torture and humiliation scares me. I replay the scene: those lengths of hose coming down on me. Then I reflect on the order to cease, that "*basta*" in Pashto the minute I implored them to stop in Italian. It strikes me as strange, an unusual reaction on their part, for torturers typically do not stop at the first cry from a prisoner under interrogation. Perhaps the flogging was staged. Our jailors must have received an order from on high. Whoever is in charge of our detention ordered them to up the ante, to frighten us. Their fury towards Sayed knew no bounds; they tried to kill him; they hold him responsible for our entry into Helmand Province and they want him to confess. Ajmal and I were treated with greater consideration: a good number of lashes but nothing that would injure us too awfully. It's a subtle distinction that will grow less so, becoming evident, pronounced, and tragic.

With the darkness and last prayers come our chains. Commander Ali and the Taliban with the satellite telephone shuttle back and forth between our hovel and a nearby village. They buy provisions and some essential items we have requested. Finally, they bring us some medical supplies: a plastic bag containing antibiotics and ointments, bandages, Band-Aids, cotton-wool, hydrogen peroxide and a little vial of iodine. Ajmal is given the task of attending to my wound. He does so with delicacy and great care. While he is cutting my hair so that the Band-Aids will stick I tell him that I'm worried about what might have happened internally, that I'm afraid a hemorrhage or a hematoma might lead to a clot. If I move my head even an inch it feels like it's going to explode. I have to stay perfectly still. The Band-Aids do not stick well to my wound and with the dust, the ants, the fleas and the thousands of insects that have invaded our kennel, the risk of infection is high. My two collaborators suggest I cover my head with a turban. But when I wrap anything tightly around my head, I feel my blood beating and the pain spreads all over my cranium. I will use the turban as a swab, protection against the rats that could be attracted by fresh blood during the night. I sleep little and poorly. I have a block of clay for a cushion. It crumbles beneath the weight of my head but I can't do without some kind of cushion. One does not sleep well on a mattress of stony ground, with one's movements fettered by chains and padlocks. I have been noticing an unsettling development: they now tend to separate the three of us, as if underlining the differences between us, dividing us into the good guys and the bad guys.

Ajmal and Sayed are chained together at their ankles. They can walk, but they must always do so together. I wear a chain a few inches long around my ankles. I can only shuffle along slowly. It is closed with two small padlocks that bite into my flesh. Unlike my two fellow prisoners, whose hands are free, a second chain fetters my hands, one that is tightened or loosened according to the ever-changing moods of our jailors. I can never understand these moods nor foresee changes in them. I understand only one thing: they are conditioned by orders that come from far away. I'm convinced that by now all Afghanistan is talking about us, particularly here in the south. There are many signs to this effect. A radio, for example, has appeared out of nowhere and we overhear BBC newscasts, in Pashto, reporting on three missing journalists. We can barely hear the report, a confused murmur that my two collaborators struggle to make out.

News of our fate is spreading. Definitive confirmation of this fact comes late that night. Darkness has enclosed the pen in which we have been lying now for several hours, the same pitch black that covers the entire area. It's Friday, March 9. We've been in the same part of Afghanistan for two days by this time. The officer with the satellite telephone bursts into the room followed by four men in traditional attire, their faces covered by turbans. It's not easy, but we stand up. With chains around my wrists and my ankles fettered, I frequently lose my balance. I lean against one of the freshly arrived guests.

They stare at us with great interest, scrutinizing us as if we were strange animals yet to be classified. I no longer hear the word "spy." It has disappeared from the dialogues that the Taliban hold while on guard duty; it is not even hinted at in front of these four mysterious men.

Ajmal and Sayed greet them deferentially, touching the arms of our guests with one hand, according to Afghan custom. You may be enemies, but when you meet one another both hands must be lifted to the person in front of you, and you mutter a few words that signify peace, welcome, may Allah guide us, pleased and honored by the visit. Even these four men squeeze arms and hands, and speak in stock phrases and standard greetings. We had been told that the leaders, the *helder*, wanted to see us. Here they are, I imagine, in the shape of these four men.

But I'm wrong. I catch a familiar word, though it is pronounced in Pashto with the closed vowels that I will eventually learn to identify: al-Qaeda. I grasp hold of whatever I can—words that crop up often in conversation, expressions, verbs, adjectives, anything that will help me intuit the gist of the conversation. Ajmal does not translate except when authorized to do so. Without the support of my interpreter, I feel increasingly isolated. Ajmal is terrified by the idea of accidentally revealing some kind of secret: among them, the fact that he is the nephew of a high-ranking officer in the Afghan police.

I'm now obliged to ask permission before having conversations translated, conversations that seem connected to our condition as prisoners and weigh upon our future. It's not easy. Now, for example, I cannot catch nuances, those details that might help me understand who, exactly, is standing before us.

The four men, their faces covered, stand inside the pen for a few minutes. Then they make their farewells and disappear into the darkness. Ajmal, frightened, whispers: "Al-Qaeda, Pakistanis." I don't know what to think. I realize that Ajmal is following his intuition. I ask if they are the famous leaders, the ones who wanted to meet us. He says he doesn't know; he's convinced that they are local leaders, and that they come from over the border. We will never see them again. Indeed, for the entire duration of our captivity, we will never see foreign fighters: no Chechens, Arabs, Bosnians, none of the so-called international jihadists. We are held prisoner by Afghans. Yet the presence of these four characters confirms that we are in a tribal zone a few kilometers from the border. The Pakistani city of Quetta, a center of Taliban activity, must be just beyond the mountains hanging over us. We are in the heart of their territory.

I ask Ajmal about this when darkness falls, whispering in his ear. But he's afraid. He doesn't want to reply. He says I have to trust him: "After I'll tell you all the important parts. They're suspicious of us, every time they see us or hear us talking they ask me what we've been saying, they expect an instantaneous translation." I am silent. I close in on myself once more and try to make some sense of all this. I'm afraid that Ajmal knows more than he admits, that he's developing an assessment of our situation that is different from mine. He has decided to listen rather than talk. But he has also decided to tell me only what is essential.

I close my eyes and try to sleep but I can't. My mind is again overwhelmed by a tempest of thoughts, hypotheses, and considerations. I have committed many things to memory: details, sounds, and smells. As I often do, I begin to run over the opening of the story I will write about this incredible, impossible adventure. I reread it a dozen times in my head. The sentences flow clearly and smoothly; the periods, commas, and adjectives are all where they belong. I'm surprised: I'm thinking of the piece I'll write even though my hands and feet are in chains, even though I am a prisoner, merchandise to be exchanged. I imagine they are already planning a swap, or are engaged in some kind of negotiation. In the meantime, the mere idea of one day being released and writing the article instills courage in me; it helps me overcome what is perhaps one of the first truly difficult moments of our captivity.

I hear a loud chirping inside our pen. We have a sparrow that comes in and out of our hovel constantly. I interpret its presence as a sign. My wife Luisella, who is Italo-Peruvian, once explained to me the symbolic meaning of some occurrences. Birds signify change; they are messengers bringing news of a turning point, a development of some kind. The thought comforts me in this moment of extreme desperation. I feel her close to me. I delude myself into imagining that she is here with me, that she has come to deepest Afghanistan under the guise of that sparrow. Perhaps she wants to send me a message of hope, or make me understand that I am not alone, that she is actively studying the right moves to make. Above all she wants to convey serenity. And this she does. Whenever I manage to close my eyes the dream is almost always the same. And so it is now. I fall asleep and dream of her.

The Taliban bring me cigarettes, a packet of SS 80s, Korean made. I will never be without something to smoke. I thank them, but I am distrustful. The flogging they gave me still smarts, and this pain encourages me to be prudent. A gift, a small consideration on the part of our jailors cannot be confused with kindness. It almost certainly hides another trap. The game is demanding and it must be played with shrewdness. Ajmal continues to use the same tactic, acting the part of one who is offended, sick, and depressed. He is closed in on himself, his head hanging down, and his languid eyes fixed on an indefinite point somewhere in front of him. He tries to make our jailors feel pity for him.

Sayed, on the other hand, is loquacious, taking advantage of the relaxed atmosphere to talk with the Taliban. I don't know what he says, Ajmal refuses to translate and every so often he glances reproachfully at Sayed, shakes his head, and returns to his self-imposed isolation. He often rebukes Sayed when we are together in the cell. He says he talks too much, that he contradicts himself, and that in this way he increases the suspicions of our kidnappers. He says the same thing when we're alone. "He's writing his own death sentence." He whispers: "They're collecting information. Sayed is from Lashkar Gah, he knows this region. They will soon know everything about him. It's different for me. I'm from Kabul, it will take them more time to get accurate information." I turn to him and ask, "Are you afraid they'll discover that you're the nephew of a police officer?" He shoots me a terrified look and tells me to be quiet. He says that they may be able to understand what I say. In fact, he's convinced that the man with the satellite telephone understands English perfectly though he pretends not to. "You too," he continues. "Sometimes you are imprecise, when all that is needed is some small doubt to set off an alarm. You have to explain your answers carefully." I ask his pardon, and ask myself, though my strategy has been different from his all along, if he's right. But then I remind myself that I have nothing to hide.

They wake us at seven. It's Saturday, March 10, the sixth day of captivity. I ask the time constantly and thus manage to follow the rhythm of the days. We're on the move again. Finally, I think, we'll be leaving this hole behind us. I'm pleased. I prefer movement because the time passes more quickly. I ask if our journey today will be a long one, but the Taliban give me only a vague answer. The pickup is ready. As always the fighters sit on top of one another in the cargo bed—their weapons leaning up against the side rails, the rocket launchers loaded. I find it difficult to get used to my new arrangement: the chains on my wrists hamper my movements, leaving marks and bruises on my skin. It is a damn uncomfortable position that I barely manage to tolerate. Ajmal tells me the commander has spoken to him about an investigation that should take about five or six days. Perhaps they have already obtained the information they were looking for. There's a new Taliban in our midst, young, like the others, his face framed by a short black beard, his eyes dark, deep, his gaze inscrutable. He helps me up into the cargo bed and asks about my wound, my state of mind. Then he introduces himself: "My name is Tariq."

Ajmal doesn't trust him. During a break in the journey he warns me to be careful: "He's from al-Qaeda, from Pakistan, he understands English perfectly but pretends he doesn't." I'm worried, but also puzzled. I sincerely doubt that Tariq is part of bin Laden's network. I have run into them a couple of times, in other theatres of war: their faces are full of hate; they want nothing more than to see you dead. Tariq, on the other hand, is a mild-mannered man. He is educated and intelligent—completely different from our jailors. I learn that he is a pious man, a religious scholar; he studied for many years at the Madrassa. He knows the Qur'an by heart and he is always reciting it. But it is the topics we touch upon—he in his labored English—his open-mindedness, and the absence of any form of fanaticism in him, that convince me Ajmal is mistaken. He will acknowledge these qualities the following day, when he says, "Tariq is an anomaly in this context. He seems like a true believer, a man of piety. He is cultivated and blessed with a depth of knowledge that is rare among the Taliban."

We head back the way we came, leaving the maze of gorges behind and winding our way around the mountain ranges. We're heading north. My heart's beating like mad. I remember well our journey to the south and I follow every move the commander makes at the wheel. We're heading back on the same routes we took to get there, those used by smugglers; then there's the stretch of desert, the two mountains that marked a new phase of the journey. I smile in a way that I have not smiled in two whole days: we're going back, I think. Something has happened. Our detention has taken a new turn. The change announced by the sparrow last night has perhaps come to pass. I need to believe this.

Tariq is sitting beside me. Unlike the others, he's not cradling a Kalashnikov in his arms. I believe he has a role that's different from the others, perhaps he has been brought into the group to obtain information. My first hypothesis proves false, and my initial diffidence, amplified by the almost paranoid suspicions of Ajmal, will be diluted as the hours pass. As he himself confesses when I ask him why he isn't armed, Tariq is a fighter, a marksman, an expert in rocket launchers. I picture him in battle, loading the rocket with his seraphic calm, taking aim and blowing an enemy tank to smithereens. He stares at the landscape through his smallish sunglasses, his straight pointy nose punctuating a face that is lean and elongated; his hair is long, dark, slightly copper-colored, and when he smiles I see that his teeth are brilliant white. "If you're here with us now," he says in his awkward English, "it means that Allah has decided it. He wanted to give you a sign, let you see the beauty of our land and acquaint you with our customs; he wanted to submerge you in the profound significance of the jihad. I know, it could have been different, but remember: behind every event in one's life, even the worst ones, there is a hidden meaning. And it's usually positive. I'm convinced Allah brought you to southern Afghanistan so that you could see firsthand the Islam of the Taliban."

Mahmud, a small, jumpy Taliban full of wit, who loves to provoke me by calling me Tony Blair, observes the conversation between me and Tariq from the center of the cargo bed. Tarik and I speak at length, but Mahmud is not concerned: he trusts his comrade-in-arms completely. He has grasped the sense of our conversation. "Have you ever seen a landscape like this?" he says, making a wide sweep with his arm. "There's nothing like it anywhere in the world. This is the land of the Taliban." He's right: the view from the pickup, moving as always at full speed, is one of rare beauty.

I think once more about the absurd situation I am living through. In a way, I'm doing exactly what I would have liked to do. I'm finally in the midst of a group of mujahedeen Taliban: I live, speak, eat, and sleep with them. I have gone well beyond a simple interview. I touch their life with my own hands and see it with my own eyes. I understand their expressions and study their customs. I am in a privileged position, but the price is extremely high: I am a prisoner, a hostage who doesn't know whether he will come out of this alive.

I vent my frustrations with Tariq. I explain this paradox, this bitter twist of fate. "I would have liked to do this as a free man.

I don't understand why you've arrested me and why you hold me captive. Was it really necessary? Now you know who I am, none of you believe anymore that we are spies. You've discovered that I am a journalist, excellent merchandise for an exchange. And this has caught even you unprepared."

Tariq smiles. He grabs the edge of a blanket that's flapping in the wind and pulls it up to my neck. He extracts a long yellow turban hidden under the pile of sleeping bags and quilts and, with extreme delicacy, wraps it around my head. Then he unwinds it and does the same thing again, careful to be sure I'm following his movements. Finally, he adjusts it a little and makes sure that it is not wound too tight over the wound on my head. He looks at his work, satisfied, and the other fighters applaud.

We travel for eight hours straight with only occasional brief pauses in the middle of the desert to satisfy our bodily needs, gulp down a prepackaged snack, gather water from large natural springs to quench our thirst, and perform prayer rites, which must be observed with a certain regularity. We cross the Helmand River at the same point, on the same little barge. I hide beneath the covers again and suffer the same anxiety, fearing that I will be overcome by an attack of claustrophobia.

I adapt to everything, obey their orders, which I am now able to foresee thanks to a kind of coerced complicity. We stop just before the sun sets for the second to last daily prayer. This one is performed as a group and presided over by Tariq. I don't know our location but they ask me often where I think we are, especially the highest-ranking among them, the one with the satellite telephone, who rides up front in the cab. I look around and mention regions and provinces which I imagine are far from here. I want to allay their suspicions. Kandahar, Herat, even Iran.

My questioner smiles and looks around at the others,

bemused. *"Iran?"* he says. I nod and they leave me alone, visibly satisfied that I have no idea where we are. In truth, I have memorized routes, directions, details, symbols, reference points. We have been moving north, but we are still far from Lashkar Gah. Thus far we have not so much as crossed paths with a single British or Afghan patrol.

The area that has been chosen for our nightly stopover is covered with opium-poppy fields and channels of running water. The vegetation is denser and the hills are rock and sand, typical of desert zones. Commander Ali doesn't trust the trails, he takes long detours and makes risky maneuvers; he charges up high ridges, coasts down steep slopes, the pickup slipping and skidding, makes swift U-turns, the tires screeching, and finds himself bogged down in the sand at least four times. We've already blown two tires and as the pickup struggles out of the most recent rut a sharp explosion announces that the third has bit the dust. The commander gets out of the cab, scratches his head, looks at the flat tire and, in desperation, pulls out a small battery-powered air compressor. The mujahedeen have already taken up scattered positions on the peaks of the rocky hills that surround us. The commander stands there watching the pressure gauge as the needle slowly rises in the edgy silence. They make us get out of the pickup. Everyone, myself included, is concentrating their energy on getting out of this situation, which is ridiculous, almost grotesque, but extremely dangerous.

The sound of several pickups in the distance puts the soldiers on alert. The man on lookout duty up on the most distant hill whistles, then makes the sound of a camel. It's a military convoy, probably British. It is the first and the last of such convoys that we will see over the course of our captivity. And it's not particularly close. Two mujahedeen shove me down onto the sand and gesture me to keep quiet. I obey, my heart pounding hard once again. There are a few minutes of extraordinary tension. The tire has been inflated. We all jump back into the cargo bed and the pickup heads off in the opposite direction of the convoy, entering a gorge formed between three high sandy hills.

Darkness has fallen and we stop for the night. We sleep out in the open. The soldiers feel safe and decide to light a fire to cook dinner—the usual potatoes with beans and some hot tea. Ajmal, Sayed, and I prepare our bed: a red straw mat and three blankets. Sayed and Ajmal are still chained together by the ankles. My hands and my feet are fettered. The chill night air impregnates the chains and my wrists freeze overnight. My ankles are protected by the socks I've been wearing for six days. I try to sleep. I calculate how many cigarettes I have left. I smoke sparingly. It is a miracle just to have them, here in the middle of the desert. The sky is the usual black mantle illuminated by astonishing constellations. But I am depressed, downcast. I have to get used to the idea of a long and difficult captivity. I leap on every new development, each new twist or surprise, anything that will inject me with a little faith, a little hope. I need a sign, some contact with the outside world. I have to know there is someone out there who is working to get me released.

Contact with the outside world is made while I'm trying to sleep. The man with the satellite telephone comes over to us, wakes us up, and with Ajmal's help asks me: "Is you wife pregnant?" I look at him, surprised. Not that I know of. But it's a strange question. I give him a little more to go on: "We would have liked a daughter, but we already have four children, two each from previous marriages. We've given up on the idea of having another." The officer puffs air out of his cheeks, frustrated. He reads a note on a piece of paper he is holding in his hand and continues: "What were you going to call this new daughter?" I tremble with cold and emotion. I swallow, only now grasping the meaning of all this: they're looking for me, they want confirmation that they're in contact with the right group. There are always many profiteers in the wings, particularly when there's a kidnapping in course. I gather my strength. "Antaya. We wanted to call her Antaya." The man with the satellite phone repeats the name, making sure he's got the right pronunciation. He walks away, calls someone, then comes back to me, radiant. "Antaya," he repeats. "Good, very good."

The mujahedeen scattered on the sandy hills, hiding in ditches dug in the earth behind jutting rocks or stretched out near the fire listen in almost religious silence. Then they explode in a cry that echoes within the walls of our open-air prison: "Antaya! Antaya! Antaya!" They yell the name joyfully, almost as if they were celebrating a birthday or intoning a hymn. This name has brought us a ray of light. There is hope for negotiations, freedom, a prisoner exchange, something, anything, planned and proposed as one part of a package determined by others, elsewhere, in the world from which I am isolated but which continues to turn. That world has mobilized a marvelous network of solidarity that I cannot even begin to imagine. I am moved to tears. That name, Antaya, reaches into the depths and touches me to the core. It was a secret between my wife and me, an overwhelming desire that we dreamed about for days and nights. It strikes me right in the heart. It is a name that will resurface often during my captivity. It will become known throughout the Taliban territories.

The party for Antaya leaves us all dazed. It is Sunday, March 11. We have only slept for a few hours, and badly. We wake up late and the sun is already up. The happiness of the night before has vanished, and I am once more assailed by a sense of oppression: I cannot get used to always having my hands bound. When it is time for tea, still wrapped in my blanket, before the fire, I find myself unable to repress an outburst of anger. I refuse to eat breakfast and, offended, I turn my back on Tariq, who sits there with my cup of tea and a piece of stale bread in his hand. The Taliban observe the scene and draw closer, alarmed but respectful of this bitter petulance of mine. They ask me quietly what has happened, why I refuse to eat. Ajmal translates, and, my voice steely, I explain: "I'm tired of having my hands in chains. I cannot accept this kind of treatment. I'm a journalist, not a soldier."

Tariq allows me to vent my anger and then tells me that my hands will soon be freed. He takes a little container of tiger balm from his jacket and rubs it on my wrists. That icy massage does me good, the cream softens my skin, which is bruised by the metal rings. I'm not the rancorous type, I've never been able to hold a grudge for long: I drink my tea and eat my piece of stale bread.

Commander Ali is under the pickup working on the damaged tire, which is flat again. The air compressor has added to the damage, for now the Toyota's battery is dead. We're on foot, isolated, in the middle of the desert. I raise my eyes to the sky, smile and think about my father. He passed away last summer, but now, like any self-respecting sailor, he is rendering the lives of those who have wronged me difficult. He has released sand storms, made it so we get stuck in the sand, punctured three tires and now he's left the pickup with a dead battery, immobilized.

But the Taliban have friends and supporters everywhere. They are overlords of the territories they control; they police the districts, arrest people, issue sentences and apply them in public according to the dictates of the Shariah. In addition, they mediate conflicts and contrasts on social questions and matters concerning private interests. The inhabitants accept this role and they help the Taliban in difficult moments. All it takes is a telephone call and within an hour a tractor shows up with a local farmer at the wheel.

I stay where I am, lying under the blanket, completely hidden from sight. The farmer makes a couple of maneuvers, yelling in a husky voice that I will hear again when we reach our next prison, the seventh. After a few fits and starts, the pickup roars to life.

We're off again, heading north across stretches of virgin desert. We climb a group of hills and from the top of one we observe a farm—two large houses and a barn in the midst of a vast opium-poppy plantation. There are a few cows grazing in a field and a flock of sheep in a corral. We coast down a long steep slope, once or twice the pickup nearly flips, and finally come to a standstill in front of the doors to the barn. The soldiers get down, stand around in a circle and make a lot of hubbub—they don't want us to be seen by this small community. As soon as I get down from the cargo bed they order me to cover my face with a green shawl that I will keep with me for the remainder of my captivity.

I enter a room with a dirt floor, four thick walls made of clay and straw, no windows, and a hole in the roof to let air in. The Taliban pick up a large straw mat, green with white embroidering, and roll it out on the floor. We sit down along the wall, transforming the barn into a living room where we will eat and sleep together. I crouch down in the corner furthest from the door, well hidden. I don't say a word or exchange greetings; I am impassive even in the face of remarks, laughter, and curiosity that concern me directly. Inevitably, I attract the attention of the farmer and his children, both the older ones and the youngest ones, who run back and forth between the farmhouses and the barn with trays full of tea, sweets, and bread soaked in camel's milk.

The farmer is obliging, he asks about the war and the battles in the north, on the frontline. It seems his sympathies are with the Taliban. But Ajmal, in one of the rare moments when he seems relaxed and less closed within himself, explains that the farmer is actually afraid. "These people don't play around," he says. "They showed up and told him, without mincing words: 'We're going to stop here tonight, this room has been requisitioned; prepare something for us to eat.'" The farmer had no choice but to obey. In their eyes, he is meek, resigned to his role, and perhaps this is why they allow me to reply to the questions he repeatedly puts to me. Again, after a long respite, I hear the word "spy": it's an explanation, a justification our jailors no longer believe, but it still works on those who must show us hospitality.

We spend the rest of the afternoon inside the barn. Most of the Taliban sleep, others kill time cleaning their weapons. They do so with skill and dexterity: they pull apart their Kalashnikovs piece by piece, shine each with an oil-soaked rag, cleaning away dust, sand and other impurities with a tuft of wool tied to a piece of string; they recalibrate their sights, polish the old chipped butts with a different type of oil. They do not have many tools. They pass around rags and dusters without a word, engrossed in this job which they consider extremely important, treating their weapons with affection, as if they really were their partners for life. They sleep with their weapons, covering them at night with blankets and sleeping bags.

Shortly before dawn, beneath a light drizzle that almost seems like mist, the little iron door is thrown open and the big boss comes in. He is followed by another man. Everyone jumps to their feet, they salute him with great deference, their arms and hands tense, their eyes lowered, muttering the standard, ritual greetings. The leader looks at me, smiles, and introduces himself. He tells me his name is Haji Lalai, and that he is military commander of the Taliban in the central districts of Helmand Province. He has been wanting to see me for days. He conducted the investigation on me and discovered that I am a journalist. He is the puppet master, the man who holds the strings to this kidnapping. His presence, not to mention his refined manners, his way of speaking, and his knowledge of

English, confirm that the management of our arrest has been entrusted to a higher level in the chain of command. Definitive proof of this comes the following day, when the entire group of soldiers vanishes, destined for places where battles are raging and we are joined by a group of boys who are less battle-ready, virtually untrained in the use of weapons, but more expert in interrogation techniques and the handling of prisoners.

Haji Lalai, whom I will call commandant, as they do in Pashto, immediately inquires as to my condition. He takes a close look at my injury and apologizes for the treatment I received at the hands of his men. He implores me to be patient; we will be his guests for another fifteen or twenty days. "Guests," he calls us! His approach is subtle, acute, always well-mannered and in keeping with the rules of good form. He is an intelligent man with a long, slightly oval face. His black beard is carefully trimmed and combed. His glasses, with yellowish lenses, correct his myopia and protect his eyes from the sun. He is tall, lean, broad-shouldered. His hands are well cared for. He dresses elegantly in a light brown *shalwar* and always wears one of two turbans, one white, the other black and gray. Far from having lived his whole life in Afghanistan, the commandant has traveled the world. He has many sophisticated gadgets, often the most recent models. He uses a satellite telephone equipped with an earpiece, which he listens to while stretched out on his side, wearing a smile that reveals a row of perfect, white teeth.

It is time for prayers, which will be recited by one and all on the shawls and mats that cover the floor of the barn. Haji Lalai officiates over the prayer, naturally: he is the commandant. His gestures are measured and precise, with carefully calculated pauses. The rite lasts longer this time, above all the part dedicated to personal invocations.

We drink some more tea, talk for a while, and then go to

bed. The room is full. I can't sleep. The presence of the big boss troubles me. I don't trust his flattery and overweening consideration. I feel that our captivity has reached a delicate phase but I can't identify the direction it is likely to take. The Taliban take turns sleeping and standing watch. During the night I see the watch change several times. Each time it happens in complete silence, which is broken only once, when one of the boys sleeping in the middle of this makeshift dormitory cries out, no doubt dreaming of clashes and battles. "Allah Akbar," he shouts over and over again, his voice strange and fearsome. His fervor shocks me: even in their dreams these boys think of martyrdom.

THE MYSTERY OF THE VIDEO

We are mere hostages to be bartered. I need a shot of faith and I grasp desperately at those fifteen, twenty days at the end of which Haji Lalai suggested our imprisonment would be over. I pass myself off as someone well acquainted with the mechanisms of kidnappings and negotiations. I ask Haji Lalai his age, a factor that has a considerable bearing on tribal relationships. He says he's twenty-eight, twenty-nine in June. I congratulate him on his rank, on the fact that he is in charge of military operations in such a vast province; but I add that he is young, very young. I tell him I'm fifty-two and suggest that, in keeping with tradition and rules of good etiquette, I have every right to feel I deserve respect. I expect, above all, a conversation of a different tenor, based on more sophisticated reasoning, on contestations more fitting to a meeting between a man who has hundreds of soldiers under his command, and a journalist whose destiny is in play. I complain, object to the trap that has been laid for me, and ask for news about the much vaunted Taliban leader who we were supposed to interview and who has supposedly been thrown in jail.

The commandant listens but gives me no clear answers. He persists, without much conviction, in citing the accusation that has been leveled at us since the very start: we entered illegally into territories controlled by the Qur'anic student movement. I ask myself whether Ajmal contacted the right person. By now, I'm beginning to doubt everything, and I feel very much alone.

On the following day, March 12, a Monday, the big boss takes a cell phone—the latest model equipped with a small video camera—turns it on, points it at my face, and with some difficulty begins to film me. Then he examines the images he's recorded, turns it off, and slips it back into a pocket of the vest he is wearing under his green military coat. He picks up a bag that is lying in the corner. Inside there is a Sony video camera. He turns it on, but now his difficulties are even greater. I explain the main functions, notice that a small built-in flash is on, and suggest that he turn it off to improve the quality of the light and color.

I want to help: anything to hasten everyone to the negotiating table. I have to get out of this as soon as possible. I still see freedom as a possibility; I'm no longer thinking only about the risk of being killed. I'm counting on the value we have as hostages, on the fact that these people need to keep us alive: we are their ace in the hole, to be played in exchange for concrete gains. So much effort, so many sacrifices, so many men reassigned from military operations to our arrest and detention: all this cannot be in vain. They cannot afford to have their prisoners die. It would be stupid, in addition to being counterproductive. I talk to Ajmal about this as we assess tactics and strategies and analyze our adversaries' moves. Prisoner of his own diffidence, troubled by the idea of revealing too many details about himself, my interpreter will opt for a different road from mine: silence. Over the entire course of our captivity, he will feel that his life is at risk.

Ajmal displays this same diffidence even now, as he takes note of the things that the commandant wants each of us to mention during the video they are about to make. Name, surname, father's and mother's names, place and date of birth; and, finally, an appeal to the Italian and Afghan governments that they meet our kidnappers' demands.

*

Haji Lalai carefully prepares the scene: my wound has been dressed with a large piece of cotton wool, which is by now affixed to the patch of dry blood beneath it; he places the green shawl on my head so that it's not visible. He sits me in front of the main door of the barn, where my face is lit by a ray of morning sunshine. I don't understand the meaning of the message. The commandant made Ajmal list a series of requests. We discussed them and I discouraged him from the start: pulling Italian troops out of Afghanistan is impossible, Romano Prodi has already excluded it; as far as Guantánamo goes, my government cannot interfere because, like the vast majority of the nations that have signed the UN charter, it considers Guantánamo an illegal prison; there's not much hope for the Bagram military base either, given that it is run by the Americans under the guidance of the Afghan government. Our soldiers in Afghanistan, I explained, have a precise role: they're on a peacekeeping mission and cannot open fire unless under attack, and even then only if certain conditions are present. They are obliged to maintain public order and offer support to the civilian population. Their mission carries a precise caveat with it, I conclude.

Haji Lalai understands the word "caveat" very well. At the sound of it, he nods. "We'll ask for a prisoner exchange," he says without adding anything further.

I read the list transcribed into English by Ajmal but I recite it with little or no conviction. I believe I only have to transmit the visual proof that I am still alive. The name Antaya confirmed whose hands I'm in. This video will demonstrate that they have not yet killed me. They ask me to send a second message, addressed to my family. My performance is better. I try to convey serenity with a slight whiff of irony that will not escape the attention of my children.

Then it's Ajmal's turn. He reads the same list but he is more visibly anguished as he does so; his face betrays the sum total of his anxiety. Perhaps he understands better than I who we have before us.

The mystery begins a few hours later when, closed once more in our cell, I manage to hear the BBC news in English thanks to a small transistor radio given to the second group of jailors. The radio's across the room, but I can decipher what is said: my video has arrived. The newsreader reports on my appearance and my words, adding that I speak in a voice that is calm and relaxed. There is a further comment: "The tone adopted by the Afghan journalist and interpreter is much more dramatic, his face is anguished and tense."

I'm convinced, and I will remain so right up to the day of my release, that the commandant made both videos public. I will be proven wrong.

Everyone is awake when I open my eyes on the morning of our ninth day of imprisonment. I have kept track of the days: it's Tuesday, March 13. My wrists are still in chains, but the tiger balm has done me good and eased the pain. I leave the barn with Sayed and Ajmal. Our feet are chained, we walk with small steps, rocking side to side a little like ducks. Our captors are gathered around a large fire lit by the farmer. They talk loudly, yell excitedly, as joyful as ever.

The commandant invites me over with a wave of his hand. He offers me a piece of bread and a cup of boiling-hot tea mixed with camel's milk, and suggests I warm myself up. "How are you?" he asks and translates his question into Pashto, which he wants to teach me: "Shan gai?" I nod and say: "Well, more or less." But my look betrays my state of mind: I'm downcast, in no mood for friendly chats. Our detention is weighing on me and worrying me.

They've prayed already, at a distance from the barn, behind a little palm grove. We're ready to go. The journey today, they tell me, will be a long one. I pray to God with all my might—

I need Him to fill me with energy and faith. There are twenty-five of us now, traveling in two twin Toyota pickups—same color, same stripes along the body. I notice that the rear fender of the one that Haji Lalai is driving, which arrived here carrying six men, is damaged: part of the metal bumper which protects the rear end is missing. It has no license plate, the left taillight doesn't work. The fighters who have been watching over us until now pile into the old pickup. The only ones who stay with us are Tariq and Mahmud, the Taliban who mocks me by calling me Tony Blair.

The commandant gets into the driver's seat and heads off at full speed in the direction of a ribbon of desert stretching out to the north. We are finally comfortable—chained as always, but with enough space to stretch out our legs, which are padded by blankets as the pickup hurtles over bumps and potholes. Haji Lalai is an expert driver, he skillfully avoids the humps and small sand dunes. Yet it feels as if there's competition between the two drivers. At the wheel of the other truck is Commander Ali, the small round Taliban, the madman who brought us here. The rivalry is accompanied by shouts, jokes, and shrieks whenever a wild animal crosses our path. The running joke, which always gets a laugh, involves the word "ush," which in Pashto means camel. We cross paths with entire herds, sometimes numbering in the dozens. They wander free in the midst of this enormous desert dotted with small marshes and clusters of rugged shrubs. The word for camel is inevitably linked to the name of the American president. "Ush-Bush, Ush-Bush," they cry, and every holler is followed by loud and violent spitting. During Ramadan, every Muslim must free himself of saliva to avoid swallowing, but for the Taliban it is a habit that is repeated continually and accompanied by a guttural noise that I will no longer be able to stand by the end of my captivity. Every time I hear it coming, I turn aside, above all when they indulge this practice in the courtyards of our crude prisons.

We pick up speed, veer west and cut across the desert trails. In the distance, towards the horizon, emerges the profile of a large black mountain standing alone in the midst of a rocky plain. While we are driving, Mahmud draws Ajmal out on a question that interests him greatly. He asks Ajmal what the girls are like in Kabul, if he meets up with them often, if he makes love with them. He wants to know if there are really movie theatres in Kabul now, and if people watch television. He needs to compare the Kabul that he knew during the reign of the Taliban with today's Kabul.

Tariq is sitting next to me. He looks steadily at the horizon in front of us and then begins to recite a sura from the Qur'an. He knows it by heart, in Arabic. The performance lasts for at least fifteen minutes—he takes only short pauses during which he breathes in deeply. When he has finished, he leans down, bringing his mouth close to my chest, and exhales. He looks at me and explains: "When you hear these verses from the Qur'an, know that they are expressions of friendship and solidarity. I breathe all of Allah's energy into you to protect you from enemies and danger. It will help you, I'm sure of this. You will return home, you will see your wife and your children again. One day we will meet again. Your presence here is a sign, but He," Tariq continues, pointing at the heavens, "He has decided that you must tell the world of your experiences here."

In spite of myself, I am moved. I want to believe that Tariq is sincere. Ferocious and determined in battle, but otherwise capable of humanity. He hands me a strange candy wrapped in gauze to be placed under my top lip: a less potent version of the green powder the soldiers use and tuck safely away in their little silver containers. It does not have the effect of a drug on me. Instead, my mouth is infused with a strong taste of anisette. I feel strangely reassured, but perhaps it is only the power of suggestion. In any case, almost to immunize myself against Tariq's influence, or at least try to, I repeat that this is what always happens during detentions: among kidnappers there is always one who plays the role of the "bad guy" and another who acts the "good guy." It is imperative that I not forget this.

We stop for a few minutes outside a village, time enough for Haji Lalai to make a phone call and assure himself that the road ahead is free of British convoys and roadblocks. I cover my head with the green shawl; beneath it is the yellow turban which I have finally learned to tie. They ask me to hide beneath the layer of blankets. We cross a river on board a small barge. I can hear only noises, excited voices, then silence. I come out from under the blankets after ten minutes or so, as the commandant's pickup moves away, to the east. Only Sayed, Ajmal, and I remain in the cargo bed. They've disappeared, all of them, vanished completely. There was not even time to say our goodbyes. The fifteen Taliban with whom we have spent the past week have been recalled to the front. Haji Lalai will explain later that our imprisonment is costing them fresh reinforcements in the war. He hints at the fact that the division is in difficulty and matters must be sped up in order to reach a solution soon. We are still prisoners, but we are becoming a burden.

We skirt the desert, then veer north into the area where we will stay for another seven days. In the driver's cab, sitting with the commander, there are two men I have never seen. One is around thirty years old, and robust. I will discover that he is one of the leaders of the group that arrested us. His name is Ali Ahmad, military commander of Garmsir District, in the center of Helmand Province. The other is a boy, and he will turn out to be our chief jailor for the next few days.

I'm surprised: we are watched over by very few now. Probably, I think, we've entered territories in which the Taliban feel secure, where they can count on help and support. The three men in the truck's cab all have Kalashnikovs. Haji Lalai shows extreme care with his. He and his gun are never apart, and on several occasions I will have the chance to examine it close up. The butt, stock, and grip are all made of a dark wood with lighter veins running through it. The barrel is gold-plated, and flares slightly towards the end. It is Russian made, he reveals during one of our terribly long nocturnal discussions. These conversations of ours are very often clashes—hard, tense, arguments during which I raise my voice at times, or storm off with my hands in chains demanding more serious analysis, more convincing and practicable proposals, ones that may realistically hasten an end to the deal-brokering going on far from here.

For an entire week I attempt to conduct negotiations of a certain nature with the commandant: an endeavor that borders on the impossible, but which allows me to discover what their demands are, both those rejected and those met with reserve.

Ajmal doesn't assist me with translations any longer. He only conveys what is essential. I feel abandoned and I bring this to his attention several times during moments both of frustration and euphoria, during the sorrowful nights spent with my eyes focused on the ceiling of a our cell, covered in darkness and silence. He does not give an inch, ever. On the contrary, he brings an end to my appeals with a sentence that allows no room for a reply: "I don't want us to talk. They are suspicious when we talk."

We leave the desert behind and enter a land cultivated entirely with opium poppies. Acres and acres of terraced plantations, with small irrigation channels linked in a sophisticated network. I will discover only later that we are in the Garmsir and Khanashin districts, in the heart of Taliban territory. The sound of pumps bringing water from the Helmand River to the fields accompanies our journey through these lands. Small villages, clusters of houses and workshops dot the large fertile plain that is the principal source for the flow of Taliban money: they live and fight on the proceeds coming from the production and sale of opium.

Ali Ahmad, Haji Lalai's right hand, explains to me one day that Helmand is the richest province in all Afghanistan and that the toughest, bravest Mujahedeen come from these lands. Kandahar is awash with the myth of Mullah Omar, Lashkar Gah with the blood of martyrs killed in battle.

We hurtle down a series of dirt roads running alongside the poppy fields and stop before a small mosque next to a school that was transformed into a Madrassa several years ago and is now little more than a pile of ruins. The Taliban have decided to leave it as it is. For them, it is a symbol of the American attacks on the civilian population. The leaders of the group who arrested us will often remind me of this. More than once, during our moves, we will pass before this school, built before the regime of Mullah Omar.

Every time I saw it, I would think of how grotesque a form of Taliban propaganda it was. Firmly against schooling, they systematically burned school houses during their sweep of the remotest and poorest villages in Afghanistan. But there, in the territories under their control, they go so far as to exalt one school; they show it off with the singular goal of demonstrating to the world the damages wreaked on them by the enemy.

We wait for hours in front of the mosque, on the side of the road, hidden beneath blankets and covers. I feel as if I am suffocating and at a certain point I lift the blankets in a quest for air. As I do so I glance at Ajmal and Sayed huddled together, immobile, like they're sleeping. The wait is endless. Then, suddenly, the pickup's motor turns over and we begin moving again.

We head in another direction, driving down overgrown

paths that all look the same. We cross a bridge that passes over a dyke. We leave the area entirely and head back towards the desert. Then we stop. The commandant orders us down from the truck. We wait a few minutes and then another car arrives, a Toyota Corolla driven by a man in his early thirties. I will never learn his name. He owns land, cultivated with opium poppy, where there is an empty house. He's Taliban. He wears the typical gray and black turban, and dark-colored traditional attire. We get into his car with Ali Ahmad and the young jailor who joined us when the prior group of soldiers was replaced. Haji Lalai and his pickup disappear into the desert.

We reach the Taliban's house and we're put in a room with high ceilings and thinly plastered walls. On the floor there is a large mat on which we will sleep. There are even some red-velvet cushions. Tonight, for the first time, we will sleep in a place that is clean and dry. But it is a temporary prison. The group is not organized well enough to handle a long detention—they have no secure bases, they have to be constantly on the move. They fear interception, and each member is forced to change the SIM cards of their satellite phones frequently.

It is above all my presence that creates difficulties: my foreign appearance, the fact that word of my capture has spread both in and out of Afghanistan, the risk that some farmer or another from one of the villages will recognize me is growing. They must keep me in good health, feed me, attend to my wound, but also hide me from curious eyes. The five different prisons in which we will be kept over the course of the next six days will all be surrounded by high walls.

We eat plain rice with butter. It is the first meal cooked in a real kitchen that we've eaten since we were arrested. The taste—delicate, aromatic—explodes and fills my senses. That night I dream of *caprese*—fresh water-buffalo mozzarella, with its tart yet sweet taste, together with ripe tomatoes. I'm hungry, we eat so very little, and I've lost a lot of weight. I also feel like I'm dehydrated: all those many days and nights spent in the desert have dried me out.

I make a quick count of the days. It's Wednesday, March 14. The wake-up call comes, as always, with someone bursting into the room. The young jailor informs us that it is time for prayers. Ajmal and Sayed, increasingly silent, leave the cell and I am left to sleep a little longer. I feel lazy, listless, prey to overwhelming psychological and physical weariness. I have memorized many, too many details: things, objects, sounds, words. My wound is closing, but it still bothers me. As usual we drink some tea and eat some bread, for once fresh and crisp. I ask permission to leave the door to the cell open: fortunately, I'm granted my wish. My fear of an attack of claustrophobia has become psychotic. Outside there is a well-tended walled garden with little paths running through it.

Haji Lalai reappears late in the morning. He greets Ajmal and me in English, then shoots Sayed a menacing glance. He asks after our health and our well-being, explains there are only a few days left, that soon, very soon, we will be free to go home. Ajmal doesn't believe him. Neither do I, but I want to know what he means by a few days. "How soon?" I ask. He opens his arms and positions his hands about twenty centimeters apart. "We're close to an agreement." I interpret Haji Lalai's gesture to mean that negotiations have begun. Those on the other side of the table, working towards our liberation, have agreed to talk. The feared wall of silence, the utter refusal of any sort of negotiation, has not been erected.

The commandant orders his men to remove the chains binding my wrists. I can hardly believe it: for the first time after seven days of torture, I can open my arms, I can fold them, and wrap them around myself. He calls me and Ajmal outside. With the tone of an interrogator who is surprised by some recent piece of intelligence, he asks, "And Claudio? Who is this

Claudio? He called me. I'm thinking you might know him."
My heart leaps and my face brightens. I immediately think of
Ajmal's friend, the freelance reporter Claudio Franco. Ajmal
spoke volumes about him when we were in Kabul together,
busy preparing for our journey to Lashkar Gah and the interview. I've never met him, never even seen him. But it's a sign:
he called, he's trying to make contact; this is a foothold in the
outside world.

I'm happy, excited. I shake my head and wait for Ajmal's
answer. I look at him, torn between wanting to reveal their
friendship and maintain this secret. I elbow Ajmal, urging him
to speak. I whisper: "You know him, it's your friend Claudio
Franco, the Italian journalist who lives in London." Ajmal
remains immobile, inert; he doesn't respond to my solicita-
tions or to the commandant's question. I don't insist but my
mood darkens once more. I shake my head, surprised, embittered, tired of understanding too little about what is happening around me. Haji Lalai walks away, then returns and calls
Ajmal over to him. He puts his arm around Ajmal's shoulders
and they walk off together looking like two friends out for a
leisurely stroll.

When Ajmal returns to our room about ten minutes later,
Sayed and I note that the interpreter's face is finally more
relaxed; he is almost smiling, his eyes shine with the secret Lalai
revealed. His translations are increasingly rare, cautiously measured according to the prevailing mood and his sense of what I
do and do not need to know. I will learn to read his facial
expressions in order to determine how dramatic certain
moments and decisions concerning our fate are. It is anything
but easy.

The same thing happens now. The interpreter remains
mute, and doesn't share with us what he has learned from the
commandant. Later, I discover the reasons for his silence:
Sayed has been found guilty. With no explanation, he is

removed by the commandant himself and taken away. Ajmal is worried. He tells me that Haji Lalai considers the two of us clean and thinks that Sayed is the real problem. "He talked too much and he was full of contradictions," Ajmal adds, torn between joy for our temporary absolution and anguish for the sentence hanging over the head of our friend. "I told him over and over, I advised him to explain only what was essential. He didn't listen. He talked and talked."

I ask Ajmal what he told the commandant. Ajmal raises his eyebrows and replies firmly: "Naturally, I denied ever having worked for the British, as they seem to think. I told him that Sayed's clean, too, that I know him well, that he only helped me get in contact with the Taliban on various occasions." I interrupt him: "Why didn't you say that you knew Claudio? He is an important contact, if he called the commandant it means that he has a message from outside, they want to use him as a messenger." Ajmal looks frightened. "I can't tell them that. I don't want them to know who I know and why. The less you say the better."

I say nothing. I find his answers unconvincing. Once again, I don't understand. I'm worried about Sayed: recently, his silences have been growing longer and gloomier, I don't know what's going on in his head, how he's holding up. It's not easy for us to communicate due to the language barrier. When Ajmal and I are alone, I begin to think aloud. "In the best of cases, they'll rough him up a bit. But I'm worried they're going to kill him, that we'll never see him again. And we will meet the same fate, sooner or later." Ajmal's mood has grown dark again. He nods, silently.

The following day, March 15, we change prisons. The owner of the house in which we slept last night is afraid. He feels the foreign and Afghan secret services breathing down his neck. My interpreter confirms this fact. He overheard some exchanges outside our room. "He's mostly afraid of the consequences," he says. "One day, we will be free, and we might be able to recognize him." This thought freezes the blood in my veins. I suddenly realize that all the Taliban have shown us their faces from the start. This detail, certainly not a minor one, can be interpreted in two ways: they have decided to kill us no matter what, or they are already wanted, their faces known to those who are looking for them, and our being able to identify them makes no difference at all.

We're moved to a nearby house, a kind of farm with two large square central buildings, a spacious tree-filled courtyard, three verandas with thatch roofs, small fields and gardens enclosed by high walls, and two towers at either end of the property. It is not a fortress, but a small, abandoned farm. We will stay here for two days and two nights, watched over by nine very young Taliban fresh from the Qur'anic academy—devoted, pious, ready to obey every order. The hierarchy becomes clearer when I learn that our detention is managed by a mullah named Maulvi. He is about thirty years old, tall and robust, with a thick dark beard. He is a teacher at a madrassa. I will have dozens of discussions with him about religion, especially Islam, to which he will attempt to convert me time and time again, but without excessive zeal. He is convinced that success in this endeavor would gratify him as much as a martyr's death in battle.

I try to converse with these boys. I ask about their lives, their habits. At first they resist, but slowly they begin to respond to my questions. They tell me about their origins, about the ambitions and passions that animate them. We speak in gestures, with occasional words and phrases translated by Ajmal and the few words of English they have learned who knows where. They seem open, willing to exchange ideas. But when it is time to flog me, they will feel no compunction.

Punishment arrives without warning. The chains come back out. They take them off, put them back on again, close the door to my cell for hours on end, loosen and tighten the chains around my ankles. They flog me, just a few lashes, for no apparent reason. I'm convinced that these choices are made on the basis of how negotiations are going, that they do not represent anything personal, that every action corresponds to a precise order given by the leaders of the group that is holding us prisoner. Tolerance and discipline alternate continually and the days seem endless, each one the same as the last. We spend them for the most part sitting on steps of dry mud and straw, surrounded by clouds of dust and the rubbish scattered throughout the courtyard.

But our jailors' youth encourages a particular relationship between us. I interpret some of their gestures as concessions in my favor: the radio on during news hour and the way their facial expressions change when news of our kidnapping comes on; the fact that we share the same food, boiled potatoes, with beans drowned in tomato sauce; their increasingly frequent offers of tea over the course of the day.

I realize now that I have been eating out of a metal dish that is different from the others. I imagined that this was a gesture of courtesy toward a foreigner, but Ajmal explains that it is because I am a kafir, an infidel. The same segregation will be applied to water as well: in order to avoid causing controversy and bringing upon myself further punishment, I must be very careful to drink and wash using the small canteen they've entrusted me with, which is distinguished from the others by a differently colored top and a mark on the handle.

Contact with non-believers is to be avoided. It is a sin. Religion dominates everything. Prayers are said five times a day in a liturgy that is followed to the letter. Maulvi is curious about my origins, my birth in Pakistan, and he continually puts my spiritual fortitude to the test. But during our conversations there is always a great deal of respect shown for our differences. We are both interested in these differences.

To kill time, the Taliban play five-a-side football using a small ball of plastic by now reduced to a formless, unidentifiable object. Every so often one of the boys sticks the point of his knife—the favorite weapon of the Taliban—into that stiff lump and reshapes it so that it will roll better on the stony, littered surface of the courtyard. They face up to one another, bump up against each other, free themselves with heel kicks, passes, and give-and-go moves that amaze me. They laugh aloud, never complain, never protest even when fouls against them are obvious.

I'm surprised by the fact that they play at all. During the Taliban regime, in addition to prohibitions on every kind of distraction—TV, cinema, books, music, all considered symbols of western perdition—the leaders even went so far as to prohibit kites, which until then had constituted the real national pastime. Now I watch these Taliban playing football in front of Maulvi, who observes them with satisfaction, and commandant Haji Lalai, who shouts, eggs them on, shares their enthusiasm, smiles, and hugs them, these boys who are heading straight into the heart of the jihad. His sudden displays of tenderness make him seem like a protective father. They organize a mini-tournament and ask me to referee, the only role I can perform given that my ankles are in chains.

They follow my instructions and abide by every one of my calls. When I ask them why they are allowed to play soccer when every other form of amusement is strictly forbidden, they reply as one voice: "But this is football!"

We are in need of a signal, of something that creates pressure around the negotiating table. In the afternoon of March 15 Maulvi bursts into a cell and orders Ajmal to translate his words. He looks hard at the interpreter, whose face contorts and hints at a repressed sob. My heart is in my throat. "You have to make an appeal," Ajmal says in a weak voice. "There are only two days left, then they kill us." I stand up, take the satellite telephone from the mullah, and put it to my ear. I realize that there is no one on the other end of the line—evidently I am to record my appeal. I'm apprehensive, my voice is grave, dramatic: "You must do everything possible, you have to accept the Taliban's conditions. We have only two days left. I repeat: two days remaining before they assassinate us."

Our captivity has taken a turn. Time is running out. Everyone, first and foremost the Taliban themselves, want to end a game that is becoming too difficult, too exhausting. The Taliban need to get their fighters to the front, they can no longer afford to keep them assigned to our imprisonment. Two hours after the telephone call a young man arrives at the house. His name is Luthar and he introduces himself as an aspiring journalist. It isn't at all clear who he really is. They have given him the job of managing relations with the media. He holds a video camera as he leads me from the room to a field behind the two central buildings. We make a short video, the second. The camera zooms in on my face and I address the Italian government and the parliament. I take a few minutes to think about what I will say and decide to address my message directly to prime minister Romano Prodi.

Behind me, the Taliban fighters stand in a circle, their rifles and machine guns leveled at me, their faces covered by the ends of their turbans. The scene is powerful, threatening. We are hit by gusts of wind full of dust and sand that accentuate the already dramatic atmosphere. After little more than an hour, the cameraman asks me to make a third video. My appeal this time is even more intense. I address the Minister of Foreign Affairs, Massimo D'Alema. I'm increasingly alarmed at this turn of events. I don't understand why they're asking for so many videos in quick succession. They demand a fourth video. The atmosphere is extremely tense. This video will be sent to the editor-in-chief of *La Repubblica*, Ezio Mauro, to the Journalists' Association, and to the National Press Foundation. I implore my colleagues to do something. I say that it's is not just a matter of saving our lives, but a question of freedom of the press and accurate information. I ask them to do everything possible to obtain our liberation. The Taliban do not prompt me in any way; I am the arbiter of my own fate.

I speak in English, then in Italian. The cameraman nods. He doesn't look particularly satisfied but he says the videos are fine and that they will be sent, but he doesn't mention where or to whom. I imagine they are destined for TV, but it also occurs to me that they might be sent to the government, to those people involved in the negotiations. I return to my cell and as they close the door behind me, anguish and tension overwhelm me. Again, I feel as if I am suffocating.

Friday morning, March 16. Haji Lalai returns. He's calm. He invites Ajmal and me to share breakfast with the others. We discuss various subjects. I listen, reply when questioned, but I am more worried than ever. I reproach myself for the openness I conceded my jailors. I must continue to distrust them. I cannot delude myself into thinking that we're on the verge of a breakthrough, that we will soon be freed. I play around, talk, distract myself, but I have a knife pointed at my throat. I feel that I'm about to collapse. My body and mind are about to give.

Execution by the River

The presence of the Taliban cameraman Luthar comforts me. I try to consider him a colleague, to create a kind of tacit solidarity. He may be capable of understanding my position, the importance of the interview we wanted to do, and the error, at least in terms of their image across the world, that the Taliban are making by holding us captive. I concentrate on his professional sensibilities and insist. He speaks a few words of English, I can talk to him directly and ask him for a more precise picture of what is happening. The videos he shot, the dramatic message—two days left before they kill us—that I left by telephone, clash with the serene atmosphere of only three days earlier. "Has something gone wrong?" I ask. "They can't agree? What are the latest requests? Withdrawal of the troops, prisoner exchange?" The storm of questions overwhelms Luthar and he will only reply vaguely. He wants to be frank but cannot discuss things that are being decided elsewhere, he says. I'm certain that even he is only following orders that come from the Taliban leadership. Our case is in the hands of the Supreme Shura, led by Mullah Omar, the Commander of the Faithful.

Luthar speaks frequently with Ajmal. Both their faces are serious; my interpreter listens and nods resignedly. I ask Ajmal to translate, I try to follow their conversation mainly through the expressions on the face of my interpreter.

Commandant Haji Lalai is sitting on a large bedspread in

the center of the courtyard. With him are his lieutenant, Ali Ahmad, Mullah Maulvi, and the boys who act as our jailors. We are once again called outside and invited to join the group. Today we will eat together. Only Sayed is missing. It's been a day since he disappeared. They've brought me two packets of cigarettes and a sack of oranges, which I expressly asked for: I was feeling a desperate need for vitamins. Oranges are a rarity in Helmand Province, their cultivation is largely confined to northern Afghanistan and finding them here must have proved difficult. There are a toothbrush and a tube of toothpaste in the shopping basket. Finally, after ten days, I can brush my teeth. I do so twice, three times. I look at myself in a little hand mirror that the commandant himself pulls out of his pocket. I have bags under my eyes, my wrinkles have grown more pronounced, they've become furrows that line my hollow, tormented face.

Haji Lalai also has a gift for me: an MP3 player. On it, there are one hundred and fourteen suras from the Qur'an, in Arabic. The translation of each sura is displayed on the device's small screen. The commandant hands it to me, encourages me to use it and to follow the translation on the display. I listen to it for a few minutes: it distracts me and helps me to relax. I notice that our curious warders are fascinated by the gift, which they consider a rare privilege.

We eat the same old potatoes with beans, scooping them up with pieces of bread. My stomach is clamped shut and I'm unable to swallow a thing. I take a few more bites then turn to the oranges, which I savor. I take advantage of this luxury, for I doubt I will have any more. There are two oranges per person, and they're distributed to everyone. We eat, we drink some water and then tea, talking all the while about our lives. Maulvi presses me on the criteria adopted by our justice system and on the nature of our sexual relations with our partners. The argument revolves around simple, almost schematic, principles. There is much interest on the part of the Taliban—they desperately want to understand the social norms in the West.

Haji Lalai listens carefully. The boys, respectfully seated at a distance from the group's three leaders, remain silent, their heads hung low. The mullah asks me what the punishment is for murder in my culture. I explain that we have a penal and a civil code, that taking the life of another person is considered very grave, both ethically and morally. Maulvi insists: "But what kind of punishment does your religion reserve for such a crime?" I try to make a distinction, explaining that there are so-called mortal sins for which we must answer before God. I add, however, that in our existence here on earth murderers are subject to man's justice. There is first a trial, then a sentence, and both are based on codes that dictate a certain number of years in prison for the crime of homicide. We are against capital punishment, I add. And there are extenuating circumstances, specific situations. I conclude by saying that in our society forgiveness has an important role, even in the sentencing of a criminal, even one who has committed homicide.

I emphasize the idea of a separation between religious and civil institutions. Maulvi is engrossed. He weighs my words and finally replies: "Things are different here. Religion is the State. Our laws are all written in the Qur'an. If a man kills another man, the family of the latter can, indeed must, execute the killer. If they are unable to do so, we take care of it. We go and get him, and we execute him publicly, in the square, before the eyes of everyone. This house," he adds, making a sweeping gesture that encompasses the entire property, "belonged to a murderer. Now it is at our disposal and at the disposal of all who have need of it. Solidarity is very important to us. We help the weak, the infirm, the elderly, widows, the worst off.

"The same thing happens when a man steals," Maulvi continues. "His right hand is amputated. If he is caught in the act of stealing he loses his left foot as well. It serves as a warning. Around here there are no thieves or murderers. People circulate late into the night, the stores can stay open, the houses have no need of alarms or guards. We live happily, serenely. We feel protected."

"Is there no such thing as a pardon," I ask. "Is the idea of forgiveness precluded?" Haji Lalai replies: "These things exist. But they are entrusted to the relatives of the deceased or the victim of a theft. If they invoke clemency, the guilty party is safe. He is free. But we make certain he commits no more crimes."

Maulvi still has a lot of questions. He asks how we make love, when, and how we behave toward our partners when they are menstruating. If we wash, how many times, before or after intercourse. I respond matter-of-factly, avoiding anything that will offend their sensibilities. Western society, in their eyes, is depraved. Their questions are not the fruit of mere idle curiosity but a search for confirmation. My arguments in favor of the West hinge on the question of freedom of choice, a privilege that our world has earned with sweat and blood, with thousands of battles both won and lost; the price has been suffering and division.

But what really torments the Taliban is AIDS. They consider it a threat and combat it with extremely rigid rules of behavior. Sex must only be engaged in with one's partner. Anyone who violates the rule of monogamy will be stoned. "This is the only way to avoid disease," says the mullah. "Where you're from, the rules are unclear, they are open to interpretation. There is a lack of certainty. That's why you are surrounded by murderers, thieves, betrayers; it's also why couples in the west fall to pieces over the most minor difficulty. People do not feel safe." Haji Lalai sighs: "And for these reasons, you are doomed to eternal darkness." There is silence. We reflect on a debate in which the two sides are unable find points in common, points of contact. The differences are exacerbated by fundamentalism and fanaticism, which allow no room for debate. Their certainty is a pillar that holds up an entire social and civil structure. Any doubt, even the smallest one, would bring everything crashing down around them.

There are a dozen or so oranges left. We share them in an atmosphere that grows increasingly relaxed. One piece of orange peel is thrown, then others; there is laughter, friendly jibes, jokes, then a small battle erupts. Before long, the courtyard is covered in what is left of the fruit. I have neither the strength nor the desire to participate in these festivities. Our lives hang by a thread—it's not our party. As the last pieces of peel fly, the satellite telephones begin ringing again. I stand up and am immediately invited to remain where I am. I don't catch what is said on the telephone.

Out of the corner of my eye I see a figure approaching. I turn with a start—my heart is in my throat again. It's Sayed. Sayed, who disappeared almost twenty-four hours ago, is back. He has been shut inside the commandant's pickup all this time. I observe him: his steps are short, the chains are still around his ankles, his hands are tied behind his back, a large white strip of fabric covers his forehead, exactly like those the Taliban fighters wear. His face is swollen, his white *shalwar* stained with dirt and dark patches that could be dried blood. I am relieved: they have beaten him, tortured him, but he is still alive. I stand there with my mouth open and my mind overrun by thousands of thoughts.

None of the soldiers so much as even looks at him. His presence is normal, just as his disappearance was. But what surprises me most in that moment is my recollection of a reply one of the boys, the most mature, the best prepared both physically and militarily, gave me when I asked him about Sayed. He had mimed chains being broken and a homecoming of sorts. "Home," he said. "Home, free." Seeing the driver walking towards me, unsteadily, his hands behind his back, after being blindfolded, then shut up in a cell alone, fills me with joy but at the same time it infuriates me. They have been playing games with us again. They continue to tell us countless lies. They are lying when they tell us that we will soon be free and that we'll return home; they are lying when they tell us to be patient. They want us well-behaved, well-fed, healthy. That way, they can kill us at a more opportune moment, perhaps before a video camera, thus immortalizing their crime and disseminating it as a warning. I think of Ajmal and I realize that he's right: he's Afghan, he knows these people. He has learned one lesson the hard way: these people must never be trusted. Never.

And the murder, the crude execution, comes an hour later. Luthar arrives riding a black motorbike. He's a little nervous as he explains that we have to make one more video. Yet another. The same story: an appeal, a strong one, to the Italian and Afghan government: there must be no more obstacles to the negotiations. We're on the move again. Commandant Haji Lalai has driven off in his pickup but he will return. We climb up into the back of a new pickup, another Toyota, but not one of the powerful turbo V8s. We settle down as best we can, our hands tied tight behind our backs with lengths of fabric, our ankles in chains. We look Sayed in the face for the first time after his return. He is desperate to talk. He mutters a few words that are obliterated by the roar of the pickup, but communicates above all with his eyes.

Our nine jailors are with us, together with two kids we've never seen before. The Taliban armed with the video camera is also on board. They're all hugging Kalashnikovs and heavy machine guns. We wait for at least half an hour in the middle of a poppy field: the opium poppies look like wild chicory with their pink, purple, red, and yellow petals opening atop a hard bulb at the end of a long stalk. In two weeks the bulb will be sliced open using a special knife with three blades, and overnight a white milky paste that turns dark when it comes into contact with the air will emerge. The following day it will be harvested with a small spatula and placed inside a container that the harvester keeps on a string around his neck. At the end of the day's harvest he will be disoriented due to the extremely strong odor of the opium paste. The work is well paid, they tell me: three hundred dollars for two weeks' work. All males from the ages of eight to sixty, including Taliban, are permitted to work the poppy fields. I look out aimlessly over the acres of cultivated farmland, oblivious of what awaits us.

The heat is oppressive and the wait is long. I shift positions in the cargo bed trying to get comfortable but our jailors order me to stay still, hidden under my yellow turban and the green shawl. Luthar, the cameraman, steps down from the cab and in English tells me that the video will be shot in a cooler location. We start moving again. We plough down more paths, cross small bridges, turn onto a side road, wind around a small dyke made of sand, and finally reach a deserted stretch of land on the banks of the Helmand River. I will never forget this place. I will return on other occasions, the last time with Ajmal, right before my release. It will appear often in my nightmares.

The truck stops. The river is on our right. The soldiers spread out over the dunes and along the banks of the river to make sure that no one comes near. The commandant's pickup arrives. Haji Lalai hints at a greeting with a slight movement of his hand. Sayed is about two meters away from me. His hazel eyes are wide open. He wants to tell me something. Using small gestures I ask him if they beat him. He nods. A lot. I imagine how and where. But he looks calm now. He's convinced that soon we will be free. He adds: "You and Ajmal to Kabul and then Italy, Europe. I here, I stay in Lashkar Gah." I feel a surge of emotion, and I console him. I tell him that he, too, after this terrible experience, will be able to leave Afghanistan. I promise him that I will do everything I can to get him a visa. "You too," I add. "Kabul and then Italy." We are still sitting, our hands tied behind out backs. Sayed, however, manages to draw near. He looks at me, his eyes imploring: "Car, car. I need a new car for my job."

His Corolla vanished following the initial ambush. Sayed's chief concern in this moment is how to maintain his wife and four children, with another on the way. He cannot afford the luxury of being unemployed. I am profoundly moved: in these tense moments, in which death is so near you can feel it, Sayed is thinking about work. Despite the violence and the likely torture he suffered during the twenty-four hours he was absent, the driver still has the strength to plan a future for himself and his loved ones. He is serene, and his serenity calms me, too. He must have understood something that I haven't, that I can't possibly understand. I don't speak Pashto.

Haji Lalai, his lieutenant Ali Ahmad and Maulvi, are deep in conversation on the top of a sand dune. They're alone, each of them with his back to us. They're writing something on a piece of paper. They order their men to open the doors of the pickups. They pull us out, accompany us away from the vehicles, and sit us down next to each other. They blindfold us with a piece of thin fabric. Behind me, commandant Haji Lalai is ready. Every single face, except ours, is covered with shawls and turbans.

This detail alarms me: I'm sure something serious is about to happen. The commandant reads aloud what turns out to be our sentence: "In the name of Allah Most High and All-Merciful, Sayed Agha, Ajmal Naqshbandi, and Daniele Mastrogiacomo are sentenced to death for acts of espionage within Taliban territories." I do not catch a single word, but I hear Ajmal beginning to cry uncontrollably. He is sobbing. I have never before heard him weep so.

My voice struggling to make itself heard, struggling to emerge from my throat, I ask him what is happening, what the commandant said. Ajmal can hardly speak through his sobs. He says: "They're sentencing us to death." I turn to Haji Lalai. "What's going on, commandant? I don't understand. Wait, won't you? Just for a second. There's been some kind of mistake." I try to contain myself, to remain as dignified as possible, but I can't stop stammering. I raise one knee. The light fabric covering my eyes allows light to filter through and when I tilt my head I can see out through a small slit. The scene in front of me is terrifying. I watch, paralyzed, horrified. The taste of vomit rises from my stomach, which is as hard as stone.

Sayed has been dragged in front of us. He is on his knees. Three, maybe four large men are standing right behind him. They push him down into the sandy desert floor. Sayed can't breathe. Now, they're on top of him, they turn him over and as they do so I see that the knife has already been drawn. One of our jailors holds it in his hand. I can't see the blade but I see something that cuts into Sayed's neck. A quick, neat cut. There are no spasms, no moans or cries; nothing. The scene plays out in an icy silence. Then, a hand. One of the Taliban works on Sayed's neck, front and back. Sayed's body is inert by now. His head is removed and they lay it on his torso. They clean the knife on his white tunic.

Sayed's blood does not splatter over anyone; it does not gush from his severed arteries. This is not butchery. It's worse: a barbaric and cruel rite cloaked in religious mysticism. I cannot tear my eyes from the scene. Now, it is our turn. I'm sure of it. Our chances of saving ourselves are next to nothing. The sentence weighs on us, heavy as lead: death by execution for acts of espionage. Ajmal confirms everything. He cannot stop crying. The bile in my mouth gets stronger and stronger.

The decapitated lifeless body of the driver is delicately lifted, taken to the riverbank, placed in the shallows, and pushed away on its final voyage. Luthar is not far away, video camera in hand. He is filming the closing scene. Someone comes over and adjusts my blindfold. Perhaps they have realized that I saw everything.

I'm in shock, shaken by uncontrollable convulsions. I stand up and walk towards Haji Lalai's pickup. Again I ask what is going on. I pretend as if I haven't seen or heard a thing. I wait, my heart beating madly, for my turn. I see myself manhandled, suffocated in the sand, decapitated, my body floating downriver with the current, ending up trapped in the marshes or in one of the small dykes that regulate the irrigation systems. Eaten by fish. Lost, never again to be returned to my family. I feel something touch my shoulder and turn brusquely. They take my blindfold off. Before me, I see the commandant, smiling. My hate for him rises, almost overpowering me. He is capable of killing a person and then laughing about it. He shouts some order at the boys, who have already taken their positions in the back of the pickup. They jump down and lead me with my hands and feet in chains to the truck. Ajmal follows me, trembling and still sobbing. "They're not going to kill us, they're not going to kill us," I repeat, over and over, almost as if I were prey to a mad obsession. Fear is coursing through me: death will now be our constant companion. We will have to learn how to live with it, with the idea that we might be slaughtered from one moment to the next.

We have been sentenced. The execution has merely been postponed.

WE WILL SEE EACH OTHER IN PARADISE

We have returned to our prison. I am exhausted, worn out, incapable of shaking off my almost catatonic state. I wrap the green shawl around me. I'm trembling with cold. I unwind my sweat-soaked turban and let it fall to the ground among the crumbling dry-mud bricks. They are infested with ants, spiders, strange and enormous fruit flies going back and forth between the piles of dry bread and the orange peels scattered in the courtyard. I allow myself to be colonized by this army of insects. My legs buckle beneath me, my knees are no longer able to carry the weight of my body. I fall. The chains are still on my feet, which fold beneath me like shapeless rags. I let myself go. My breathing is labored. The dry retching that began back at the river doubles me up with pain.

The air is heavy with death, blood, and pain. The old wooden door to Sayed's cell is open. I gaze into that black hole and tears fall down my dusty, dirty face into my white beard. My lips, chapped and dry, are bleeding. I dry them with the back of my hand. My arms shake. Ajmal is already in our cell, its door also ajar. He is sitting on the ground, gazing at nothing, his face ghostly, pallid, his lips trembling. I collapse onto the filthy earth and fidget with a few breadcrumbs, losing myself in the frenzy of the ants. They work without cease, surmounting every obstacle with enviable tenacity and endurance.

I try to distract myself. I have to find a way to interrupt the horror film playing in my mind. I see my driver again, the jailors suffocating him, the knife cutting his jugular, the severing of his neck. His head coming free from his body. His murderers are still here, before me. They keep their distance, respecting the silence that oppresses us. They move slowly around the thatch pergola, where the oldest of them is already at work preparing dinner. They gather around the hand pump that brings water up from the farm's well. They wash thoroughly, one part of their body at a time until they've covered everything, without, however, stripping naked. They then busy themselves with their clothes: shirt, undershirt, trousers, shawl. They go about this very carefully, scrubbing each piece of fabric, their hair, hands, face, ears, nose. They wash away every trace of blood. It is a purification rite, they are cleansing themselves, protecting themselves from being contaminated by the spy they have just executed. There is no sign of anguish, horror, or penitence in their movements. They are silent, serious. The metallic, rhythmic sound of the hand pump reigns over all.

I spend part of the afternoon collapsed in a corner of the courtyard like a bundle of rags. They let me sleep. My sleep is troubled. I am mocked by nightmares that swell up like ocean waves. A hand touches me, shakes me awake. I open my eyes. Leaning over me is the Taliban with whom I usually exercise. He has never told me his name, but now I recognize him: I realize, with horror, that he is Sayed's executioner. I despise him and from this moment forth I will keep my distance. He inspires terror in me. With a sharp jerk of his head he indicates my cell: it's time to go back in.

I'm unsteady on my feet. I lose my balance several times. The executioner holds my arm as he accompanies me to the entrance of my cold dank hole. Once there, I begin to panic. I'm facing another long night locked away in utter darkness, another restless night during which I will wake often, each time unable to step outside or leave where I am. I will wake and stare at the wooden door and wait for the first light of dawn to show through the cracks in the thick boards. I grasp hold of the idea that Ajmal and I are still valuable hostages, that the Taliban need to keep us alive, that the negotiations have moved ahead, that our deaths would render any possible exchange impossible. But I do so without conviction.

I turn things over, trying to apply cold, hard reason to my thoughts. I do so alone, for my interpreter sits there immobile in the same position he has been in all afternoon, his eyes wide open. We don't talk: there is so little to say. I finally whisper, my voice barely audible: "They have killed him." I don't know if Ajmal witnessed the scene. I imagine he did and his answer confirms this impression. "Yes, yes," he replies, his voice strained, high-pitched, muffled by his sobs, which he tries to hold back with his hand. We are anguished, depressed, desperate. Ajmal rouses himself with a start and in the same tone of voice, says, "We have only two days left. Tomorrow it's my turn, they will kill me. I'm certain of it. The next day it's your turn."

He is shaken by sobs. I reassure him, embrace him, take his hand in mine. I tell him that nothing is certain, that the macabre video they shot at the river exists only to show how serious and resolute they are. "They can't kill us," I point out. "They still need us." I am holding tight to this conviction.

Luthar, the cameraman, returns. He enters our cell as if he were not directly involved in what has happened, as if he had not witnessed Sayed's decapitation, one charged with the job of carefully recording each small detail of the event. He asks us to shoot yet another video, the fifth. He wants me to make another appeal. It's not necessary that Ajmal accompany me. I'm petrified. I don't trust him. Now, I think, my time has come. I stand up, my legs trembling. The jailors take hold of me and drag me out of the cell to the back of the main building and place me in the middle of an uncultivated patch of earth enclosed by a high wall. I'm going to die. They are going to shoot me.

They haven't blindfolded me and this makes me think that there is still a ray of hope. I have to play my last card: I address the Prodi administration together with the entire parliament, including the opposition party. I plead with my friend Silvio Sircana, Prodi's press officer. My appeal is to "our society's Christian principles." I am adamant about the humanitarian nature of our tragedy. I speak first in English and then in Italian. I look at Luthar. The Taliban turns the video camera off. Rivers of sweat are running down my back. I am picked up and taken back to my cell. For now, at least, the execution has been postponed and I am still alive. I think back to our breakfast together, the one this morning that ended in the orange-peel battle. I now see this episode under a different light: it strikes me as a kind of last meal, something that is granted every prisoner sentenced to death. Sayed has already been killed, now it's our turn.

I'm in my cell again. It is time for the fourth and penultimate daily prayer. Our jailors are eating and they wish to do so in peace, together, inside their room. We fall asleep without uttering a single word and are woken at dawn the following day by the door being flung open and the jailor on duty entering and announcing that it's time for morning prayers.

Saturday, March 17. I leave Ajmal alone to perform his ablutions and I devote myself to mine. Now, as I wash, hunched down on my ankles, which are still in chains, I pray to my God as well. This is one of the most dramatic moments of our captivity. Everything has been turned upside-down; everything is once more in doubt. We have been plunged again into uncertainty and death looms over us once more.

Time is running out for us. The ultimatum was clear: forty-eight hours and we will be executed. Staring fiercely at Ajmal, Maulvi reminds us of this fact. His look reminds me of the first time he set eyes on Ajmal, a savage gaze that literally terrorized my friend. Afterwards, he had said: "Did you see that face, those eyes? They belong to a real murderer, a cutthroat." Now the mullah says there's no more time. "Daniele has to call someone important. A minister, a senator, Prodi himself, his wife, the newspaper. He has to say that there are only forty-eight hours left, then we kill him."

I look at him, bewildered. I ask him what is happening, if there are fresh obstacles. This most recent change in their mood has left me distraught. I know nothing about what is happening in the outside world, for we are inside a bubble, where only a few vague signals reach us and guide us through the darkness. Nobody tells us anything, nobody explains. We are alone again, a knife at our throats.

Maulvi doesn't pursue the idea of a phone call. He leaves and I watch him as he walks away, calls someone on the satellite phone and returns. He yells at Ajmal, his tone severe: "What does *lapo* mean?" My friend translates the question. I have no idea what he's talking about. My interpreter repeats the word: "He said *lapo*."

I don't understand his question. Lapo is a name, and the only association that comes to mind is Lapo Elkann, the nephew of Gianni Agnelli, he, too, party to a misadventure that brought him face to face with death. But then Maulvi repeats his question this time with greater clarity. "Is it true," Maulvi says, "that you have two *lupi* at home?" Now I see what he's getting at. *Lupi*, in Italian, means wolves. I reply with haste, as if I were answering a question in a quiz show, one that might decide my fate. "No, yes, I mean . . . I have two *lupi*, two wolves, but they belong to my father and mother. The wolves live with them, at their house outside Rome, not with me." The mullah smiles, satisfied. He asks me what color they are. "One is black, the other the color of this wall," I say, and point at the mud walls of our cell.

I add some other details without being asked. I want the answers that make it to the outside world to be clear and accurate. I realize that this will serve as further proof that I am alive. Just a little while ago we were videotaped witnessing the execution of our driver. Almost certainly, this video has made its way to those people who are negotiating for our freedom. They will have seen it. Their blood will have run cold at the point in which Sayed's throat is cut and he is decapitated. They will be wondering whether Ajmal and I met the same fate, and now they want to ascertain whether we are still alive or not. I tell Maulvi that one of the wolves is a male, the other a female, that the former is bigger and his name is King, and the other, Joy, is smaller.

I am overwhelmed by a storm of emotions and fears, my mind is terribly confused, and for a moment I struggle to remember the name of the female. It comes to me after a few desperate seconds. In order to be sure that everything has been understood and that the message will arrive clear and accurate, I write the two names down on a page in the mullah's agenda. Everything, in that moment, seems to be of supreme and decisive importance.

Maulvi walks away to communicate my answers via satellite. One of the Taliban calls me outside. He wants to listen to the suras from the Qur'an on the MP3 player I was given by Commandant Lalai. I have not grown fond of it in the least. The buckets of blood, the countless horrors on the hands of these murderers cloaked in religious piety disgusts me. I give it to him and tell him he can keep it as long as he wants. I watch him walk outside with the earplugs in his ears, his lips moving as he recites the Sacred Book. He is engrossed, submerged in this moment of spirituality. I will never see him again. I'll ask about him but they will tell me only that he's left, called back to the front. Knowing he might easily die there, he asked me for the device in the hope that the verses from the Qur'an in Arabic would fill him with courage.

We change prisons, the fourteenth such prison in thirteen days. They wait for night to fall before moving us. The interpreter has overheard some of the soldiers saying that the trip will be short: we will probably remain in the same area, Garmsir District, the heart of Taliban territory. The commandant, his lieutenant, the cameraman, the owner of the first house, the one who cooked us rice, all arrive at once.

Our transfer is not an easy matter. The tension is high; I believe they suspect there has been some kind of interception because they've been on their satellite telephones all evening. Spy planes have been rumbling overhead more often than usual. Every time they pass, our jailors raise their eyes skyward with worried looks on the faces. They tell us to remain where we are, covered. And whenever we're invited to get a bit of fresh air, to indulge in some exercise, we must stay near the wall, under its sloping roof. And the hard, watchful eyes of our jailors are always upon us.

We leave this most recent prison in a Toyota Corolla station wagon and Haji Lalai's pickup. We drive for half an hour along a small dirt road full of holes that runs alongside one of the principal irrigation channels. The night is pitch black. I can no longer see the stars that I have so often admired in the desert. The fields are covered in a fog that is caused by the water-filled canals and the small marshes that dot the acres and acres of opium poppies.

We stop in front of a black gate, get out of the trucks and walk down a small dirt path. We enter a first room, open at the front, with three walls and a roof that is partially collapsed, where several Taliban whom we have never seen before are

preparing a bed. They tell us to keep going and we enter a second room, larger than the first. It looks like some kind of store-
house: clean, larger than our previous prisons, a high roof held
up with large iron columns and wooden cross-beams that have
been painted and lacquered. I note that each of the wooden
beams has two words written on it: "Metaldis, Karachi."

The place lifts my spirits a little. "We'll be all right here," I
say to Ajmal. We examine the mountain of objects that fills
much of the large room. I stop before the back wall. Behind a
pile of shovels, spades, picks, grain sacks, buckets, and other
tools, there is a small wall of dark-colored bricks. I move closer,
swaying from side to side because of the chains around my
ankles. I take a closer look: they're shrink-wrapped bricks of
opium. Maulvi, who has poked his head into our new cell, picks
one up and says, "Two kilos, each brick is two kilos of opium."
Good business, I say. How much does each cost? "Three hundred," replies the mullah. "Would you like to take one with
you?"

I decline his offer. It's really the last thing on my mind. And
above all, I see in that apparently innocuous question yet
another trap.

We make our beds on the hard earth floor. We have more
space now. Sayed's absence, the emptiness his passing leaves
behind, is palpable, more so now that in the twenty-four hours
they held him isolated before cutting his throat as if he were an
animal. After his disappearance, the interrogation, the violence
and the torture, he was brought back to our prison, but they
closed the door of his cell. He only came out again to meet his
physical needs, to which he alerted the jailors with a voice that
became increasingly weak, lost, inhuman—the agonizing cry of
a wounded animal locked in the depths of black, lonely hole.
The scene of his death comes back to haunt me. Ajmal's gaze
tells me that he, too, is replaying the same scene. It's something

we will never be able to forget. We abandon ourselves to sleep, our bodies and minds exhausted.

Sunday, March 18. The entire day passes without a single verbal exchange. Maulvi and the gang of jailors respect this mourning ritual we are observing, but they're worried. The idea that we might fall ill, or perhaps even fall into depression and let ourselves go, troubles them. If we die it would mean a whole load of trouble for them, too. This idea has begun to tease our tired minds. We want revenge, we want to make things difficult for them. The only weapon we have is rebellion, to no longer play the role of submissive hostages, to begin a hunger strike.

In the afternoon, the executioner arrives and mimes some stretching exercises, inviting me to get some exercise. I need to move; my leg muscles are weak and atrophied. I accept his invitation, but without much enthusiasm. I'm worried above all about Ajmal, who has finally emerged from the cell. His breathing has become labored, he holds his right hand against his heart, and his face is pallid. I ask him if he feels OK. He tells me, his voice weak, that he's having palpitations. He leans against the wall, his legs fold beneath him, and he slides slowly onto the ground. I lift him up and tell him to walk, holding him up. I try to distract him, telling him he must do a little exercise to help his circulation. Fear, tension, the questions to which we must always give a measured response, the presumed or real secrets that we must be careful not to reveal, the effort needed to provide information that may or may not prove decisive, all these things have worn away what little strength we have left.

Ajmal is agitated. In an urgent, strained whisper that conveys both enthusiasm and alarm he says: "I've discovered incredible things. Now I know who the Taliban are, how they're organized, how they move, where they live, where their bases are. I have listened to everything that our jailors have said." Now I am alarmed, too. Ajmal could turn out to be a very inopportune witness. I ask him what he has discovered. I'm worried, very worried. He shakes his head: "Not now, I'll tell you later." Then, with a smile that is supposed to instill hope and courage, he says: "I'll tell you everything when we get back home." I insist: "I should know, too. I need to understand. We're in the same boat and that boat is threatening to sink. It's no longer a question of keeping your sources and their secrets to yourself. We have to keep studying our adversaries, develop a joint strategy. We have to stay unified. If they manage to separate us, to turn us against each other, it's over."

In our new prison we sleep very little and poorly. We hear the squeaking of mice beneath the mountain of tools and sacks. When night falls and the room is in complete darkness they become brave and draw near. I feel their feet on my face and swat them away with little or only temporary effect. As if it were the most normal thing in the world, Ajmal tells me that the mice are running all over his body. "I cover myself well, feet and head included," he explains. "And I let them do whatever they want. After a while, they go away." I can't do it. I cannot sleep knowing that rodents are free to frolic over my body. The injury on my head is healing, the wound has closed, but sections of the scab covering it fall away regularly leaving traces of fresh blood that attract the mice. The idea of waking up to mice licking or perhaps gnawing at the gash in my head terrifies me.

Maulvi hasn't been seen since he left with the information about my family's wolves. The persistent and threatening request that I make a telephone call in order to avoid having my throat cut has been left in limbo. This waiting makes me nervous and Ajmal, with his hermitic silence, doesn't help. The mullah returns right before sunset. He has brought us a small battery-powered table lamp, which we will use to keep the mice at bay, pointing the beam of light at the mountain of tools and buckets. Later, he bursts into our cell and shakes us from the sleep into which we had finally, mercifully, fallen and picks up the subject of the telephone call where he left off. He orders me to call an "important" person.

I reflect for a minute, trying to think of someone who might be able to unblock the stalemate: Prodi, D'Alema, my wife Luisella, the newspaper. I point out that it's Sunday, a day of rest in the western world; it will be difficult to find somebody, offices are closed, even the editorial offices of the newspaper stay closed until three in the afternoon on Sundays. Isolated from the rest of the world, I cannot even imagine the exceptional mobilization of people and resources that our situation has provoked. I don't have my address book and because of the new technologies to which we are all slaves, I don't remember numbers that should be familiar to me. All my important numbers are contained among the contacts on my cell phone, I explain. "You have it," I remind the mullah. "You took it from me when I was abducted."

This is the word I use, abducted, and I repeat it, making sure my message gets through. The idea that they arrested us is a banal and absurd excuse that no longer has any basis. Even the Taliban leaders, who so carefully maintain their image of freedom fighters no longer accuse us of espionage. Ours is a classic kidnapping. We are nothing but merchandise to be traded and it is this trade, which by now has been decided almost down to the last details, that's making our jailors skittish.

Maulvi hands me the satellite telephone, something he has never done before—a gesture that demonstrates precisely how little time we have left. In large part our destiny hangs on this telephone call. The mullah is furious, his face and eyes brimming with pure hate. If he were entrusted with the chore of killing me, he'd do it without a second thought, and he would do it willingly. "Tell them that your ambassador in Afghanistan has to move," he commands me, his face hard and uncompromising. "If he doesn't put some pressure on Karzai's government I will slay you, and you know how. Do you understand?"

I remain silent, my throat dry. I swallow with difficulty. Death, by now, has become an obsession. I imagine the scene all over again: my severed head, my body, decapitated, left to rot in some godforsaken place. I see it all dozens of times. I hold tight to the hope, the only one I have, that I will be able to buy time with further telephone calls. I will call hundreds of people, thousands of numbers. I'll call everyone, anyone. We must attempt to save ourselves at any cost.

I take the phone from him, my hand trembling. Think, I tell myself. Who do I call? First, I phone my wife, at home, as if it were an ordinary call on an ordinary day. Nobody picks up the call. The answering machine clicks on and I hang up annoyed. "She's always out," I say. I try the hotel we own, which is managed by my brother Alessandro. The receptionist answers and when I ask for my brother she tells me that he's not in. I fling a silent curse, then raise my eyes to heaven and ask God, to whom I have been clinging ever tighter, to forgive me. I'm getting nervous, impatient; I fear that I won't be able to get through to anyone. But I try again. I call the newspaper. The telephone operator answers, and immediately puts me through to someone. I'm surprised that there are people at work this early on a Sunday morning. I haven't the slightest notion that my imprisonment has provoked an incredible battle that my colleagues and friends at the newspaper are waging incessantly. Later, I will have occasion to learn more about this battle and to appreciate just how exceptional these colleagues and friends are.

Somebody answers. I don't even give him the time to identify himself. I start in on him immediately, my voice determined. "Listen to me. You have to call the Italian ambassador
in Kabul and tell him to do everything possible to move the
negotiations forward. I'm not exactly sure what the problem is,
but the Taliban are not going to wait: we have one day left,
then they kill us. Do you understand?" I roar, angry. On the
other end of the phone I hear a weak voice asking me, "But
how are you?" "Don't worry about that. Call now." I hang up.
Maulvi has already snatched the telephone from my hands and
is nodding, satisfied. Only after I have been released and have
returned to Rome, will I learn that the voice on the other end
of the line belongs to the managing editor, Angelo Aquaro. He
kept the sheet of paper on which he wrote down my instructions and gave it to me upon my return. He confessed that he
was shocked by my call. The stress and tension had been growing steadily over the fifteen days of my captivity, involving an
increasing number of people and my call had arrived at the
height of it.

Night falls. It is time for prayers and another dish of potatoes in sauce that I can't even touch. Right then, news of our
fifteenth transfer arrives. The Taliban keeping watch over us
have been showing signs of both remorse and fresh concerns.
Fragments of sentences, words in Pashto that I have learned to
recognize . . . there is talk of a blitz. The idea alone is enough
to terrify me. I'm against any kind of armed intervention in
cases of kidnapping: the hostages always get caught in the middle. These men do not think twice about murdering or being
murdered. For them death is synonymous with liberation, not
mourning. They spend this mere flicker of earthly life waiting
to die in battle and ascend to paradise—their reward for having participated in a jihad in Allah's name.
And yet the risk of a raid carried out by the special forces

of some nation or another—perhaps British, for Her Majesty's armed forces have long been active in this remote province of southern Afghanistan—inspires prudence in our warders. As soon as darkness covers the opium poppy fields we are on the move again. There are two vehicles in our convoy, the Toyota station wagon and Haji Lalai's pickup. Four armed men join our group. One of them is older, around thirty. Our hands are bound again, mine in chains. We get up into the pickup's cargo bed and head down a dirt road that runs alongside the two principal irrigation channels.

As usual, the stereo plays strains of Taliban songs. The voices and the melodies are infantile, sentimental. Two tears fall down my face, signs of desperation. I am going to die, I say over and over again. I'm not going to get out of this alive. I think about my wife and kids, who are grown by now, but who remain, in my mind, defenseless babes to whom I have never given enough. They will be even more fragile and vulnerable following my death. I rebel in the presence of these thoughts and with all the strength left to me, all the accumulated weight of my desperation, I make a proposition to the commandant: if I must die, I want to die fighting.

My request is serious, and I expect a serious reply. He laughs and in English, a language he knows well but pretends to have difficulties with, he says: "You will return home. You will see your wife again and your children." I swear to myself that I will not let them cut my throat; I will revolt and they will have to shoot me. I will not give them the satisfaction, and when I see that terrible moment approaching, I will escape. I will be killed by a blast of machine-gun fire, maybe even shot in the back. They will be shocked and they will not be able to immortalize the scene that they are so looking forward to with their video camera.

The convoy stops in the middle of nowhere. There is an

intersection a hundred meters away. The commandant and his second in command get out of the truck and walk away from us. Once they have gone a certain distance they stop to talk with a man who apparently has been waiting for them. We remain where we are, in the middle of the road, the silence broken only by the croaking of frogs. The air is humid, heavy. The three men walk back together towards the truck and point a small flashlight in my face. The beam of light passes from my face to that of Ajmal's and then back to mine. The new man has a limp. His face is covered by a light blue *patu*. He pulls it away from his face: long, messy black hair sticks out from the bottom of his turban. He has a bristly beard. He doesn't smile, doesn't speak. But he keeps staring at me. I only need to see his eyes to recognize him, for I have studied his photos for hours: it's Mullah Dadullah, the real commander, the architect of our abduction, the rebel, the ruthless leader that we were supposed to interview, as many had before us, less than three weeks back.

My heart skips a beat. Anger, not fear, swells in me. Rage at the plot against us, the trap into which we fell, planned and effectuated by someone who stays in the shadows and plays with our lives, pursuing objectives that we don't know, that we cannot even begin to imagine. Something too big for us, insignificant hostages struggling for our lives.

"Thank, thank you," says the leader, extending a hand that I cannot bring myself to shake. Thanks for what, I really do not know.

My blood boils. I interpret those words as yet another provocation aimed at bringing about my complete psychological collapse, another attempt to get a reaction out of me that would furnish them with an excuse to humiliate and hurt me further. My smile, which is closer to a sneer, is nothing if not a suppressed roar. I fill his face with insults and curses that echo inside my drained, exhausted body.

Dadullah even tries to be funny, adding: "In the end, you have obtained much more than an interview. You have seen how we live and how we think. Do you think yourself capable of telling the truth about us? You journalists never do." I don't reply to this further provocation. His presence alarms me: I'm convinced that we're on the verge of some kind of turning point. Ajmal is mute, his head hung. He raised his eyes for an instant, enough time to reach out and greet the mullah with the same deference he shows everyone. Nothing more than good manners on his part, certainly not fondness. He's already understood whose company we're in and the discovery is like a cold shower. We have been used, sold out, mocked, fooled. It fills us with bitterness and makes us feel impotent, almost ridiculous.

Just as swiftly as he appeared, Mullah Dadullah vanishes in the maze of paths that cut through the fields of opium poppies, and is swallowed by the dark night. But before leaving us, he turns to me and adds in a voice that is almost a growl: "You owe your life to our supreme commander. It was Mullah Mohammed Omar himself who suspended your death sentence. He decided not to have your head cut off." Ajmal is paralyzed by fear. We both are. His voice, as he translates, is barely audible. I think I understand what he said, but I ask for confirmation: "He's talking about Mullah Omar?" My interpreter nods, his head lowered, his chin almost touching his chest and his hands tied behind his back. I reflect on this latest revelation while my heart beats hard. I wonder if this might be the latest in a long line of lies. If not, if it is the truth, then I have been had another reprieve. The damned knife that appears in my dreams every night is still in its sheath. But I have no way of knowing how long it will stay there.

There is still a long stretch of road to travel, over bumps and small bridges, past dykes, clusters of houses, and workshops built with sheet metal, small villages of tents and huts made of straw, brushwood, and cardboard dotted along the edge of the desert, down paths that cut through the fields of opium poppies and lead God knows where. Everything is cloaked in darkness, submerged in the night. Electricity has not made it this far, not yet at least, although the Taliban do not suffer because of it. Their world remains shackled to the past. They dream of a society that follows in the footsteps of Mohammed, a great emirate that embraces the entire planet; an immense oasis of peace ruled by the sacred Book, the only one that can save humanity, they repeat often, and reward every pious man with Paradise.

Around me I see only poverty, dust, dirt, and very few females, all of whom are covered in long black tunics. They move quickly down the village streets, as close as possible to the outside walls of the houses and buildings. I see children, boys, and men preparing for the opium harvest armed with Kalashnikovs and rocket launchers.

We stop in front of a large country house surrounded by high whitewashed walls. The entrance is nothing but a small narrow door, so low that one must bend down to enter. We pass through the door and emerge into a garden in full bloom. There is a tool shed, a stall, a pen and a central structure made up of two large rooms. There is a crowd here, maybe thirty people. Our jailors have been joined by twenty or so Taliban from other parts of the province. They're all armed. Their control over us has been tightened once more.

Ajmal is completely closed within himself. He has difficulty translating what our captors say. He tells me that his head hurts so much that it feels like it's going to burst: he has gathered so much information, memorized thousands of details, discovered a world that he didn't even imagine existed, one that is completely different from what he thought he knew when he was in Kabul, a thousand kilometers away. I believe he has thought long and hard about what is happening to us, about errors he may have committed, about who might have laid this trap for us. He inspires tenderness in me: he is suffering, he feels as if he has been betrayed, and, perhaps, as if he is the victim of a game that is much bigger than us and that we don't know how to get out of.

We sleep. The morning wake-up call is the same as ever. Breakfast is the same. Morning prayers the same. We're tired, awfully tired. At this point we are on the brink of a complete mental and physical breakdown. I ready myself for yet another day without books, pens, amusements of any kind, or friends. We are alone. We don't even speak to each other anymore. We pass the entire day in a kind of daze, stretched out on the quilt we've been dragging around with us for two weeks. I ready myself for another seven days in captivity. I don't know if I can resist, but I must. I think of other kidnappings and make a few calculations: the average is about twenty-five days. We need more time, the people trying to save our lives are working on finding a solution. We don't know who they are, but surely someone is on the other side of the negotiating table.

The leader of this gang of jailors once indicated a virtual length of time by holding his hands about twenty centimeters apart. The distance between one hand and the other grows less every day. Towards noon, the distance is little more than a hair's breadth. And at two in the afternoon, right after the collective prayer, nothing separates one hand from the other. Maulvi comes into the room where we are sleeping and for the first time ever he is smiling. "It's done," he announces. "We are very close to an agreement." After half an hour Commandant Haji Lalai arrives at the compound. His presence troubles me: he is the bearer of tidings that will either decree our deaths or announce our release. We hear the roar of the Toyota, his voice in the garden, his footsteps on the concrete footpath in the courtyard. He pulls open the sheet of plastic nailed to the wall that is the door to our cell. I look at his shining eyes, his brilliant smile. He opens his arms. "Two hours. Get ready. You're free, you're going home."

Ajmal and I remain immobile, refusing to believe his words. We fear being deluded once more, for we can no longer believe in anything or anybody. We no longer trust our own shadows. The word "freedom" is no longer part of our vocabulary. We have eliminated it as a form of self-preservation.

But it's true. They release us. The mujahedeen that have held us prisoner for the past seven days burst into our cell and send up an excited, contented cry. They're happy, radiant, they congratulate us, shake our hands, hug us. We stand there like blocks of stone, not reacting to these demonstrations of affection. We consider them part of a fresh trap, theatrical gestures to which our imprisonment has made us accustomed. We reject them entirely. But the Taliban insist: they take a large stone from the garden, place it beneath the padlocks on Ajmal's chains. They start hitting them with other stones and awls. Two of them work on the locks. Then they're joined by a third. A fourth and more experienced man offers advice and finally picks up the tools himself and, more methodically and with greater precision than his fellows, he continues striking the padlocks for almost half an hour. The padlocks must be broken, they can't be opened with the keys: the group that captured us near Lashkar Gah lost them somewhere in the middle of the desert.

I look at Haji Lalai. He's on the telephone again. I ask him to be clear and sincere with us. "You're free," he repeats, looking me straight in the eyes. Finally the large padlocks on Ajmal's ankles break open, and, not long after that, my rusty padlocks, smaller but full of dust and earth, are busted open. For the first time in two weeks I can actually walk, take long strides, bend my legs, open them. I can even run—I had almost forgotten I was ever capable of doing so.

I run around in the middle of the garden dragging Ajmal with me, forcing him, yet again, to get a bit of exercise with me. He resists at first, as he always has, but then goes along with it and finally I see him smile. His grin gets wider and wider until he begins to laugh and to cry. Tears, rivers of joy, roll down his cheeks into his beard, onto his shirt and chest. We unite in a long embrace. We're free! They let us wash and change our shirts. Mine is still dirty with the blood I lost after they struck me with the Kalashnikov. Now, the Taliban want to show the world that they treat their prisoners well.

Haji Lalai is in a hurry. He looks at his watch and says, "Let's go." Two mujahedeen that I have never seen before accompany me to the exit and put me into a Toyota Corolla station wagon. Haji Lalai himself is at the wheel. Beside him is his lieutenant, Ali Ahmad. They put the chains back on my wrists: a precautionary measure, they explain. We're in the final stages of the kidnapping, and the smallest hitch could send the whole thing up in smoke.

I turn towards the house as Ajmal emerges. He makes a gesture of victory: he raises his arms over high his head, his hands still chained. I will repeat this same gesture when we land at Ciampino before the crowd of colleagues and officials who will be there to welcome me. It is a public tribute, a gesture of immense joy at having won the battle that we waged over two weeks of terrible imprisonment, and a grateful acknowledgement of all those who did not give up on us.

Haji Lalai drives us through poppy fields, across bridges and past intersections. We're heading for Helmand River and I feel anxiety mounting within me. My hands are tied, there are two mujahedeen, one on either side, blocking my exit. I fear that our liberation has been staged, that we've been lied to yet again. I don't know who to trust, where and how the exchange will happen. Nobody tells me anything. Only Luthar, who has appeared out of nowhere, confirms that I will soon be free. He has his video camera in his hand and he carefully records everything: our exit from the farmhouse, the brief journey, the caravan of vehicles hurtling through poppy fields. The whole thing is under the expert direction of Haji Lalai.

We stop several times: in front of a cluster of small bodegas that look like places where some kind of food is prepared and perhaps sold; near a house full of Taliban, armed to the teeth and awaiting orders. The atmosphere is electric. Everyone's nerves are on edge. They are continually in contact via two-way radio—no one uses the telephones anymore.

We're still heading towards the river and we've entered the same tract of desert where our driver was executed. Panic stiffens my muscles and I feel as if I'm in a straightjacket. There are all the ingredients for another trap: the scene is set, the Taliban journalist has his video camera, the soldiers are armed, their faces covered with shawls and turbans. That barbaric murder, preceded by just such a scene, occurred only three days ago and it could happen again now. The death sentence for acts of espionage has been handed down; it just needs to be executed. It is not a remote hypothesis, rather, something concrete that could happen from one moment to the next.

The convoy stops a few meters from the riverbank. The leaders of the group get out of the car and sit down beneath a small cluster of palm trees. They watch the horizon through binoculars. They speak on their two-ways and wait for answers. The wait lasts at least two hours.

Then a signal arrives. They get back in the vehicles and we begin moving again, but back in the direction we came from. We trace a long wide arc and return to the banks of the river

Helmand at another point, about three hundred meters away from the site of Sayed Agha's execution. The Corolla heads straight for the river and stops in front of an iron barge.

On the other side of the river there are dozens of men. Behind me forms a long, compact phalanx of armed men. They run to join us, coming out of nowhere, pulling out rifles, rocket launchers, and large-gauge machine guns. I am in the middle, feeling, even now—now more than ever—like vulnerable prey. I don't know what I'm supposed to do. I crouch down on my heels behind the barge.

I'm afraid that they might start shooting. I ask, my voice little more than a whisper, "Who are all those people on the other side of the river?" The commandant replies in English. Finally. He speaks it perfectly. He lied to me to the very end. "Friends, they're friends," he says. I don't trust him. "They're soldiers, but whose? Afghan? Italian? British? They won't start shooting, will they?" Haji Lalai reassures me, but his men are getting more and more agitated, and he knows it. They're moving too close to the riverbank. They want nothing more than to shoot, to fight, but there's nothing against which they can hurl their accumulated rage. "Stay back and don't fire," says Haji Lalai. The soldiers obey. They stop dead in their tracks. They oversee the process. From a distance.

We board the barge. First two, then three Taliban board with me, then more, until the iron barge is full with about ten Taliban. It twists to one side—at that point in the river the current is strong. The barge is hand-operated; it's necessary to pull a cable that connects one side of the river to the other. A few minutes pass during which many hands grasp the vibrating, shuddering cable, during which I remain seated at on the floor of the barge. They finally take the chains from my wrists. They tell me to keep my turban on, to keep my wound, which is still dressed in band-aids, covered.

The minute we touch the other shore they pile out of the

barge. There is rejoicing, a tangle of embraces, many smiles, loud greetings. It is completely chaotic: they touch me, they hug me, they bounce me from one to the other.

I'm free. I'm really free. I smile and think of Ajmal. I can picture him somewhere in the midst of this desert, unchained and ready to leave for Kabul. "I know," he told me during the few confused minutes prior to our departures. "They will arrest me, they'll put me in jail. The Afghan police will want to interrogate me. It's logical enough. But I prefer that kind of prison: my father can visit me every day. I will feel protected, safe."

Somebody grabs me by the shoulders. I turn. A voice whispers, "Welcome back. You're safe now." The leaders, the soldiers, everyone, let go with bursts of machine-gun fire and blasts from their Kalashnikovs. They are celebrating a victory. I jump with every shot. My nerves are shattered. I collapse before even the slightest form of violence. I've seen too much of it. I can't stand it anymore.

Haji Lalai, the commandant, pulls me aside for the last time. He smiles with that angelic look of his and whispers in my ear: "You are a lucky man." He repeats what the man who orchestrated our abduction told me two nights ago: "Remember, you were saved by Mullah Omar himself. He decided not to cut your throat." Then, calmly, almost as if he were saying farewell and good luck, he adds, "God willing, we will see one another in Paradise."

THE MEDIATOR

The Mediator, Rahmatullah Hanefi, director of the Emergency-run hospital in Lashkar Gah, shakes me: "Let's go. You'd better get in the car right now." He has been standing at a distance all this while. Nobody has greeted him or embraced him. We leave, with a car in front of us and a jeep behind us, both carrying our guarantors: four tribal leaders who will escort us along the road back. Three hundred kilometers of desert, dunes, rises and depressions, small lakes. It's a difficult journey. The atmosphere is tense. We are still in hostile territory.

The mediator watches me in the rearview mirror. He sees my tears, watches my sobs, he reaches back and takes my hand in his. "I didn't want to come," he says. "I'm risking my life and that of my family. I did it because Gino Strada asked me to. He's waiting for you."

Slowly, I begin to understand. My eyes full of tears, I ask: "Emergency?" Rahmatullah nods and smiles. He pulls out an ID. "I'm from Emergency. Check it. Stay calm, you're safe now." Then he continues: "I haven't slept for three days and three nights. We worked hard, we didn't stop for an instant. It was really very difficult to pull you out of that hole. An impossible endeavor, but we did it. I didn't want to, I would never have come here, into these lands. The risks are great, and we are still running them now. But this is how we work: we're a humanitarian organization. For us, human life holds the highest value, it represents an absolute. We cure and we save people. We saved you and Ajmal. We would have liked to do the same thing for Sayed."

I look around, smoke in continuation, cry. I let myself go. I chase out the nightmares, release all the anxiety, anguish and pain that accumulated over two weeks of physical and psychological torture.

That hell is now behind me. But another authentic hell is yet to arrive. It will strike me in waves, hour after hour, as surprises, shocks, arrests, ferocious arguments, and threats arrive one after the other. And at the end of all this comes the final devastating blow: the death of my Afghan interpreter. He will be held prisoner for another fifteen days, then his throat will be cut, he will be decapitated, perhaps as part of the same ritual that befell our friend Sayed. Betrayed by the Taliban, by himself, by someone who was playing with our lives in a game that was bigger than any of us could know.

There's time for the penultimate daily prayer, the one that precedes sundown. The sun is setting in the west, disappearing behind the sand hills. The sky is red and orange, long purple ribbons in the sky announce the coming of night. Rahmatullah has already laid his mat out and is facing Mecca. The tribal chiefs arrange theirs beside him. They pray in silence following a rite that I have seen many times during our captivity. I pray too, at a distance. I thank my God for the fact that I am alive; I thank him also for Ajmal's life. I think back to my friend, I ask myself what he's doing right now, who will accompany him to Kabul. I remember how afraid he was these last days, when euphoria at the possibility of our imminent release alternated with moments of profound distress. I always tried to avoid slipping into the well of depression. I exalted every grain of hope that came our way. We continued to hope, because hope was the only way we knew to resist.

I ask Rahmatullah if he has any news of my friend. I speak quietly, glancing left and right warily. I still do not feel secure, we are in the middle of the desert, in Taliban territory. They could still stop us, attack us, abduct us again. The idea alone is enough to strike dread in my heart. I'm not sure I could endure anything like that. It would be another awful shock, the latest of many.

The mediator does not reply. He gets back into the car and invites me to do the same. We're in a hurry, the sky grows darker by the minute. Lashkar Gah is still a long way away. I look at the dunes, the large oases transformed into marshes, herds of camels drinking at their edges, and I realize that I would never have been able to leave the heart of Taliban territory alone. I am certain of it. It would have been impossible; they would have caught me immediately and probably have killed me. Even the tribal leaders have difficulty finding and following the trails that are barely visible on this carpet of stones and sand. On our left, at the edge of a long high sand dune, I can see the shapes of several armored vehicles. "English," says Rahmatullah. "They keep their distance. They watch without intervening."

The landscape changes suddenly and we finally turn onto a paved road. Small villages appear here and there, men and young boys sit near the intersections and watch us pass, their looks curious and suspicious. We stop a few kilometers outside the city to say farewell to our guarantors—their work ends here. Rahmatullah is finally able to get a signal on his cell phone. He calls Emergency and asks for Gino Strada. He speaks instead with Strada's collaborator, Gina. He explains where we are, and how long it's going to take us to get there. His first words on the telephone are: "They released him. Daniele is in the car with me. Safe and sound."

I'm riding beside Rahmatullah now, on his left, in the passenger seat. The Škoda's steering wheel is on the right. It's a brand-new model, the seats still covered in plastic. The mediator keeps shooting looks at me. He is keeping tabs on me, afraid that I might suffer some kind of collapse, that I will not respond well to all this. He's right: I'm struggling to understand what has happened to me, where I am, where I'm going to. I'm still inside a kind of bubble. I don't know anything about anything. My only sensation is this feeling of being tossed from one situation to another, as if I were watching a film about myself. It is an instinctive reaction, a protective mechanism. My mind is beginning to play strange and terrible tricks on me and I'm surprised that I still manage to resist. My approach is similar to that of my mother. I have inherited these maternal genes: when faced with immense pain, intense stress, tragedies, she keeps an emotional distance from things, which protects her and saves her. She conserves her strength so that she can react like a lioness when the decisive moment arrives. She reared five children and trailed after her husband, following him to every godforsaken corner of the world.

"Gino is waiting for you," says Rahmatullah. "He has to talk with you. He wants to explain lots of things." I turn to my right and my heart stops again for a fraction of a second: I recognize the collection of mud and straw houses we're passing. It's where they stopped us and abducted us. I point it out to the man who saved me. "Are you sure?" he asks. I look over at the houses again. Now they look like all the others. I recognize some crossroads, I think I don't know: the landscape around here is all the same. No, I'm not sure. I ask how long until we reach Lashkar Gah and the mediator answers a dozen kilometers or so. He explains that we were abducted elsewhere, not far from here, but in another zone. Our driver, Sayed, was well-known around here, his brother Mohammed Daoud was the first to raise the alarm when Sayed did not return on March 5. Our abduction was reconstructed in detail, and this is not where it took place.

A Light in the Darkness

We're in front of the gate to the headquarters of Emergency. It opens and we enter. As I get out of the car I see Gino Strada with his whitish beard and his long hair. His eyes are bloodshot, showing the signs of many sleepless days and nights, and stress. He has, as always, a cigarette dangling from his fingers. We run towards each other and I wrap him in a long, intense embrace. I repeat the same words over and over: "Thank you. Thank you. You saved my life. I'm alive. I can touch you." He holds me tight and says, "It was hard, very hard." He says he had to throw all his weight against those who were blocking the way to a successful negotiation, that he had to raise his voice; he threatened, gave in, found the strength to continue. He fought for us. "I really had to struggle to make them keep the knife in its sheath," he adds. He is lauding the efforts he and Emergency made and the results they obtained. But he deserves this moment of triumph: it is a way of releasing the tension that has built up inside him. There is nothing quarrelsome or manipulative about his words.

The telephones are ringing off the hook. The entire staff greets me. There must be twenty or more young men and women: doctors, nurses, specialists, paramedics, and technicians. Slaps on the back, handshakes, hugs, warm greetings, a quick toast in front of a table covered in delicacies, the kind I dreamed of at night in my cell. Gina, Strada's collaborator, gives me a quick checkup. She examines the injury on my head and checks my eyes. My entire body is shaking and I can do nothing to stop the tremors. They decide to give me ten drops of some kind of sedative to calm my nerves, I'm sure, but the only thing I taste is the fresh, cool water into which the drops have been dissolved. I start smoking, a lot, too much.

The few telephones that still work are white hot. The calls arrive one after the other without a moment's respite and grow even more frequent as the minutes pass. I talk to many people, mostly colleagues. I know their work well and I understand what they're going through right now: they must contact me at any cost. I first speak with the editor-in-chief of the newspaper I work for, Ezio Mauro. He says a quick hello and hands the phone to my wife, Luisella. Her voice wraps itself around my heart and squeezes it tight, then descends into my stomach, turning it inside out like a glove; from there it moves into my breast where it falls back into place like a veil coming finally to rest.

From the depths of my being rises a sadness that wholly envelops me. I weep uncontrollably, my face twisted by sobs. The young men and women from Emergency leave the room and close the door, leaving me alone with this immense sadness. I repeat, obsessively: "It was terrible, terrible, terrible." Nothing else comes out of my mouth. She hands the phone back to the editor-in-chief and I manage to get a grip on myself. He comforts me and asks if I am able to write. His question stirs my sense of pride. He knows well enough that I always complete the assignments given to me. I tell him I'm ready. To return to the world of the living I need to gain a sense of normality: writing will do me good. For the past fifteen days I have spoken little and understood even less. I have to vent all the frustration accumulated during this period of forced silence on the keyboard of my PC; I have to pour the story that changed my life into the computer's memory. I write hastily, without my glasses, which were taken from me, along with everything else, by the Taliban during the initial ambush.

Gino Strada is sitting next to me, talking about all that hap-

pened during our captivity. Out in the lobby confusion reigns.
There are photographers everywhere and right now they're
recording the video that will be put online in a few minutes. In
a loud voice, Gino says, "Here's Ajmal. He's here, too. He's
having pictures taken. Let's get him over here." I wait for a few
minutes, but I'm overwhelmed, confused, beset by emotions. I
remain submerged in the piece I am writing.

I smoke, nibble at some pieces of cheese. But my stomach
is closed tight, I need water more than anything; I feel dehydrated. I call the newspaper again and send in the piece. I'm
completely exhausted, devastated, but adrenalin is keeping me
going. I look at the clock hanging on the wall: it's two-thirty in
the morning. We decide to sleep. Tomorrow morning we'll
have to be up early for the trip to Kabul. Gino Strada tells me
that we'll drive to Kandahar with a convoy of Emergency vehicles. I don't like the sound of it; it sounds dangerous. I tell him
I'd like to think about it, but I know that I don't have many
options: those who saved my life know the best way to get me
home safe.

I sleep for a couple of hours, wrapped up in my clothes,
dressed, as I have been for fifteen days, in the green *patu* which
I use to cover myself. I wake with a start shortly after dawn.
They take me into the main room, where breakfast is ready. I
look around trying to find the yellow tea I've gotten so accustomed to, pick up a few pieces of bread, sample them and
swallow with difficulty. There are a few people already up and
about. I ask about Ajmal and they tell me that they don't have
any news. "Gino was mistaken. The person he thought was
Ajmal is a new worker at the hospital. He'd never met him and
he got things mixed up."

The founder of Emergency bursts into the corridor. He is
distraught, his hair a confused tangle, worse than usual.
"They've arrested Rahmatullah," he cries. "They picked him up

at home, or maybe along the road at some point. Maybe even here out front. We have to learn why, what they're accusing him of." He's desperate, furious. He sucks on his cigarette and blows out smoke as he paces the corridor like a caged lion. I am silent and immobile before Gino's rage, and shocked by the news of the arrest of the man who came to save me from the clutches of the Taliban. I feel that something awful is happening, that this ordeal is not yet over.

I think things over hastily. I think about the fact that I was freed, that the Afghan police are looking for me because they want to interrogate me. My position is delicate, I must move with great caution. With the Taliban I learned to trust no one, to think carefully before acting, to weigh each word before pronouncing it.

There is shouting and fighting at the entry gate. Slogans being chanted. A hospital security guard enters the room breathless and says there are at least two hundred protesters outside. Many of them are part of Sayed Agha's clan. They're asking to be let in, they want precise answers about their relative. Gino Strada is concerned. He's worried that they will break down the gate—the crowd, armed with rocks and sticks, is growing every minute that passes, they shout and beat against the large white iron gate.

The Emergency personnel and I move towards the internal garden. The security officers suggest we stay away from windows and the walls that protect us from the crowd outside. Doctors and paramedics lead me to a room. I want to change my clothes. I am not a Taliban and I have no intention of being mistaken for one.

I'm afraid. I look into the room and search it quickly for a place to hide. I feel like a hunted animal. I ask for a change of clothes. Gina, Strada's right hand, gives me a pair of brown pants. A young man who looks completely lost offers me a light gray sweatshirt. "Take it," he says, his voice choked. "You can give it back to me when this is all over." I put the clothes on as fast as I can and pick up a pair of green hospital clogs that I find in a large box. I'm wondering how I can protect myself, frantically looking around again for a hiding place. If the crowd breaks through the gate, I think desperately, I'll slide in under the bed. Perhaps they won't find me.

Outside, the crowd is still growing. There must be more than three hundred people out there by now and the police are having trouble keeping them back. A delegation is allowed to enter: four, maybe five men, some of them very young, all of them relatives of the driver. They sit around a table and talk with Gino Strada. They ask to see me and I enter the room and join the group. One of the driver's cousins goes straight to the point. His eyes are bulging almost out of their sockets. "Did you see Sayed's release?" he asks me. "Where did they take him?"

I'm dumbfounded. I realize that the video of his decapitation was never made public. Five days have passed since that barbaric murder and nobody knows anything; even his clan, the large tribe that is laying siege to us, is convinced that he is still alive. It seems impossible, but this is Afghanistan. Here, news can travel like the wind or at a snail's pace. And in the territories controlled by the Taliban only what they want to be known is allowed to leak out. The Taliban, the current overlords, the dictators of the Shariah, are in complete control of a kidnapping from which they hope to obtain the maximum political profit. They hide the horrors and exalt their successes. I no longer know what the free world knows of us, of our abduction, of our fifteen days in captivity. But I know the truth and I tell it to them.

I reply plainly, directly, my surprise evident: "They killed him before my very eyes." Their reaction is violent. They cry out and yell. "Where, who was it? You have to tell us who his murderers are." I'm frightened. I don't know what to say anymore. I don't know how to lie, especially about such an atrocious death. I look over at Gino Strada and realize that he is confused and worried. The boy in front of me stares at me, his gaze stern. He is enraged. "You tell me they killed him. You have to tell us where and who. We will now go to vindicate his death." I try to stop them. I encourage them to be calm and patient.

A policeman enters the room. Afghan, an officer by the looks of it, perhaps a captain. He smiles and settles everyone down. He notes the questions posed and answers given. I am still dazed, shocked by the idea that Sayed's family had no idea he was dead and I ask myself just how much of the truth made it to the outside world, how many of those videos we made were sent. I realize that the game is more complex, that it may even be a different game from the one we thought we were playing. The mediator arrested, news kept hidden, the anger of Sayed's relatives. I feel suddenly alone, vulnerable once again, a pawn to be used who knows how in this unending nightmare.

The tension eases, the crowd of relatives leaves wrapped in their grief and deepening pain. We wait for another two hours, shut inside two rooms with the young Emergency workers acting as human shields out in the corridor. Nobody says a word; everybody is worried. The atmosphere is one of alarm. Gino Strada appears to be searching for some solution. We have to get out of this building—even Strada agrees that it is not well enough protected. One crowd brings others in its wake. There may be groups of Taliban ready to jump into action, as well as bandits, criminals, the police themselves, who are anything but pleased with the way the negotiations went.

Rome is on the line. It's Luisella. Her voice is calm, as it always is in the most critical moments. She says, "Listen to me carefully. You must not go to Kandahar under any circumstance. You have to go to the English. They've laid a trap for you. They want to abduct you again." She hands me the editor in chief, Ezio Mauro, who repeats the same words: "If they get you again we won't be able to bring you home. Do what Luisella tells you to do."

Gino Strada abandons the idea of transferring us to Kandahar. He accepts, though he has many, many doubts, the plan of heading straight for the English base, which is about ten kilometers from the hospital run by Emergency in Lashkar Gah. The journey will be made in two phases: first we will go to the hospital, then to the British military outpost. We ask the police for protection and they put two manned jeeps at our disposal—they're waiting outside for us. We will travel in civilian vehicles, not pickups, without Emergency decals.

I get into the backseat of the sedan and throw a cover over myself. I have started shaking again. I'm exhausted and feel in danger of succumbing to a complete physical and mental collapse. I look around as if lost, disorientated, out of place, and again pray to my God that he protect me for just a little longer. We reach the hospital, where we remain, visiting the wards, for about an hour. The children—ill, injured, their gazes vacant—are cheered up by visits from the medical staff who have accompanied us here as part of our convoy.

There are few words spoken. Everyone is afraid, the situation could very easily spin out of control, and we all know it. There are many people who would like to see us dead right now. We have to get out of this part of the country now, nobody is safe here. I later learned that the siege on the Emergency headquarters lasted another five days and that the entire staff was forced to remain inside the hospital the whole t i m e . Threats by Taliban members, perhaps even by the Afghan police themselves, caused mass resignations on the part of the local staff. Nothing like that had ever happened to Emergency in years and years of activity on the ground.

We ask the police for further protection. There is a frenetic exchange of telephone calls between Kabul, Rome and Lashkar Gah, and then we go out onto the street and leave the hospital behind us. We travel ten kilometers along deserted city streets carefully checking every corner, every suspicious vehicle, every intersection—especially the intersections, where we could be hit with antitank rockets.

We get to the English post with our hearts in our throats. They open the gates but only after checking our IDs, despite the fact that they know perfectly well who we are. Finally they let us through. Gino Strada is still worried. We are met by two men, Italians in civilian clothes, who speak very little and are slightly stiff. They draw near and one of them speaks to me. "We were always there," he says quietly. "Down there with you and the others. We knew where you were being held. You were being monitored every minute." They are members of our intelligence corps. I don't reply. I don't even have the strength to smile.

Minutes pass, then hours. There are problems concerning our transfer from the military post to the nearby base, where it is possible for aircraft to land. More telephone calls, more pressure, further delays. Then, finally, a helicopter arrives and we board in a hurry, together with several British soldiers. It's a ten minute flight to the base, which is situated in the middle of the desert. There's a C-130 bearing the Italian colors on its way in. All together there are a dozen or so people in our group: me, Gino Strada, some Emergency staffers plus the two Italian military intelligence agents. Upon arrival there are handshakes, a few weak smiles that betray the tension. A group of British soldiers, their guns leveled, some of them walking backwards covering our backs, accompanies us to the rear door of the military aircraft.

We take off and fly through the darkness that has descended over all of Afghanistan. We land in Kabul, where Gino Strada would like to hold a press conference, but there's no time:

the prime minister's executive jet is waiting on the runway, engines running. I barely have time to greet and hug the ambassador, Ettore Sequi. I hold him tight. He is a friend.

The jet is small but comfortable. I am met by the two pilots. I try to decipher their gazes, to get some sense of what has been happening in Italy during our detention. In the turmoil of the past several hours I have had very little news. I know that there was a massive mobilization, one that I could never have thought possible. I sit down on one of the eight comfortable leather armchairs arranged around two small tables in the front cabin. On board, in addition to the female flight attendant, there is a man. I presume he is a member of our secret services. Both want to shake my hand. "Welcome back," they say, smiling.

The small plane lifts off. The turbo jets are at full throttle as we clear the mountains surrounding Kabul. Six hours later we will be landing at Ciampino airport, Rome. I relax, finally. My thoughts are of Afghanistan, of the months that I have spent in this country, of the snowstorms and the suffocating heat. I know that I will never come back. It is something I feel within me.

Now I am truly free. Safe. Alive. I have to write something for the newspaper. Ambassador Sequi handed me a laptop belonging to one of my colleagues, Attilio Bolzoni, still on assignment in Kabul, and a letter with some indications from my editor-in-chief. I ask the hostess if I can smoke. "I know it's prohibited," I say. "But I really need a cigarette." The captain has no objections. They close the curtain that separates the front cabin from the cockpit and offer me every kind of drink. I need water more than anything else but I allow myself a beer and a gin and tonic.

I concentrate on the article. I write everything, a spontaneous stream of memories regarding the Taliban, their life, our conversations, the fears and anxieties that assailed us time and time again. I write and I think. Perhaps I am really dreaming with my eyes open. My mind fills with images of the series of rooms in which we were imprisoned, the dashes across the desert, the rifles, turbans and dirty walls. I hear the sounds of our abduction and smell its odors.

I ask how long until we land. Three hours. I will not be able to deliver the article by hand. I'll have to send it in. But that proves impossible: the jet is well appointed but the Internet connection is acting up. My article on the Taliban has encountered one difficulty after another, and this is just the latest. The idea was simple enough: an interview with a Taliban commander. But the road has been full of obstacles, right to the very end. I ask if there's a telephone on board. I resort to what is by now an outdated method: I will dictate my piece. The newspaper can then publish it in tomorrow's edition.

I phone the call-corder and dictate the report. Those listening to me are happy, they heap words of affection on me. I hang up. I am stunned and still confused. I try to relax but the adrenalin coursing through my veins, the joy of feeling myself free and alive, alternating with moments of anguish for the violence and the blood I have witnessed, do not allow me sleep. I wander into the cockpit, talk with the pilot and co-pilot, observe the starry night and the lights of the cities dotting the land beneath us, and then go back to my seat. My head is completely empty. Exhausted, I no longer feel capable of thinking about anything. I'm caving in.

We land. The door of the executive jet opens and the stairs are lowered. I stand. I don't want to make my exit looking tense and crushed. I refuse to step out there looking like I have been defeated by the Taliban who kidnapped us. Ajmal and I fought for our freedom. We have to demonstrate this to the world, we have to proclaim our joy, and cry our pain for the murder of our driver, Sayed Agha. I raise my arms above my head. I'm in Italy again, alive. I have escaped from a slaughterhouse.

Two Years Later

My stupor lasts for hours. The airport is full of people: the authorities, Prime Minister Romano Prodi, agents from SISMI, carabinieri from the special ops division, the director of my newspaper, Carlo De Benedetti, my editor-in-chief, Ezio Mauro. And then my wife, Luisella, and my children Michele and Alice, who break the tense and awkward protocol and run to embrace me with a liberating cry as I come down the stairs. And friends, colleagues, my brothers and sisters, my mother, who always remained firm in her conviction that I would return home. I wave and embrace everyone. I need human contact, tenderness and support. I need to feel that I am alive. There's a festive atmosphere, a celebration for my rescue. This ordeal has kept tens of thousands of people holding their breath, torn between anguish at having lost me forever and hope for a miracle.

I think about Sayed, the boy I knew for only a few hours and whose throat was cut right before our eyes. An atrocious, absurd, incomprehensible death. It will haunt me during the long nights to come; I will wake with a start, in a cold sweat, my heart beating madly again. I think about Ajmal, who I imagine is already in Kabul, wrapped in the warmth of his loved ones' affection.

Two days of parties and joy as I desperately try to return to the real world, incapable of fully understanding what happened in Italy and elsewhere. I avoid asking myself too many questions: prison has made me taciturn. I try to interpret fragments of sentences overheard, allusions half grasped amid the rumble of voices I am incapable of fully deciphering. These voices now feel extraneous to me. I feel extraneous to myself. Everything appears extraneous and different. But the real storm is yet to arrive. It comes in waves that grow more and more powerful. Ajmal is still being held. They released him and then abducted him again when he was on the road back home. As they planned to do with me. Nobody was talking about Ajmal: the arrest of the mediator became a priority. But for me, the nightmare is not over. It continues, stronger than ever.

Mullah Dadullah considers himself invincible. He is arrogant, contemptuous. He sends a video to al-Jazeera and thus plays his final card. He wants to put the governments of Afghanistan and Italy in a difficult position. He wants to divide us, wound us, exasperate the relationships between our two countries. He has already lied once by not upholding his side of the agreement with Gino Strada. He makes an announcement: "Ajmal is in our hands." And then he raises the stakes: "Karzai must free a further six prisoners." Then comes the sentence: "If our requests are not met we will kill him."

A chill creeps over everything and everyone.

I try to understand what might have happened. I see the final scenes of the movie frame by frame. Our liberation, the chains being broken with blows from stones and awls, our embrace, the tears that wet our stricken faces, the promise to see each other again in Kabul, Rome, London. I see his smile as he leaves in a convoy of pickups and cars, his hands raised as he waves to me and heads off in the opposite direction.

It was mere theatrics. The same things happened many times during our captivity. With Sayed, for example, when they took him away to be tortured and told us he had been freed. The celebration turns into a drama. Then there is anguish, and finally mourning. I think back to the arrest of Rahmatullah Hanefi. I now interpret it as a form of retaliation, a vendetta being played out between the twin souls of the Afghan secret services. The mediator in exchange for the nephew of a high-ranking member of the Kabul police force. The orchestrator of our abduction makes things very clear. He has uncovered what Ajmal managed to keep hidden for fifteen days, and the fact that Ajmal is related to a police officer is an aggravating factor. He is a dangerous and inconvenient witness.

I concentrate on his liberation. I work day and night, constantly on the phone to Kabul, talking with the local BBC journalists. I write, then record an appeal that I address to his captors. I mobilize local newspapers, participate in the campaign organized by *La Repubblica*, talk to the Afghan ambassador in Italy. But the sentence has already been handed down. The trap has become a vise that is growing tighter and tighter, inexorable and unstoppable. It is Easter, April 8, 2007. The news reaches me and strikes me brutally like a knife to the stomach. I vomit the few pieces of roasted baby goat that I have eaten with my family in celebration of a day that is sad and full of anguish as it is. Ajmal has been decapitated in some deserted stretch of land. I've lost a colleague with whom I shared five years of my life and two weeks of terrible imprisonment. I've lost a co-worker, someone with whom I spent entire evenings dreaming, fantasizing about an infinite number of projects and plans.

Two years have passed. It seems more like ten. Time mends the soul's wounds and attenuates the pain associated with the loss of two collaborators, people who depend on you and to whom, in theatres of war, you entrust your life. This kind of relationship creates an indissoluble bond that no controversy, above all the kind that results from opportunism, can break. What remains is regret at not having been able to save them.

They were unwittingly part of a game that was much, much bigger than they were.

You have the chance to reflect on what happened, calmly, coolly, free of the inevitable sense of guilt, and to reflect on how and how much things have changed. In Afghanistan, Italy, America, the world. You reflect on the ways of keeping up with world events, of being a journalist, has changed as a consequence of the increased speed of information delivery and the quantity of information delivered.

I often think about Ajmal and Sayed. I know that their families are doing well nowadays. They received support thanks to an appeal organized by Italian journalists. My interpreter's young wife went back home and found work as a nurse. They tell me that she has big plans, and that she showed strength and dignity during the period of her mourning. Sayed's wife, meanwhile, was able to buy a store and a house with the money collected in Italy, and she still lives in Lashkar Gah with the five children her husband left her. She is part of a great tribe that protects her and makes sure she has everything she needs. Ajmal's brothers are scattered around the world, studying and working.

After three months in jail and the complete dismissal of all charges against him, including the accusation that he orchestrated our abduction, Rahmatullah Hanefi returned to direct the Emergency hospital in Lashkar Gah. Then he left his position and moved to Europe. The men who were released from prison in exchange for our liberty were killed in battle or were arrested again some time later. The man who did orchestrate our kidnapping, the man we were supposed to interview but who instead played with our lives in order to shift the balance of power in the Supreme Shura in his favor, Mullah Dadullah, is dead as well.

Many consider this episode merely a terrible and bloody story. I prefer to remember it as an experience that cast me down into the depths of my soul, that made me stronger, more convinced of the vital importance of many things: my relationships with loved ones, life's small everyday moments, basic human values, my profession. To have left this story prey to the memories and phantoms that have haunted me for such a long time would have been selfish. Sayed and Ajmal would have wanted me to tell the world our incredible story. I owed it to them. It was something I promised I would do.

Two years later, I have kept my promise.

ABOUT THE AUTHOR

Daniele Mastrogiacomo has covered national and international affairs for the Italian daily *La Repubblica* since 1980. He has worked as a foreign correspondent in some of the world's most dangerous places: Kabul, Tehran, Palestine, Baghdad, and Mogadishu. In 2006 he reported on the war in Lebanon between Israel and the Hezbollah. He lives in Rome.

Carmine Abate
Between Two Seas
"A moving portrayal of generational continuity."
—*Kirkus*
224 pp • $14.95 • 978-1-933372-40-2

Salwa Al Neimi
The Proof of the Honey
"Al Neimi announces the end of a taboo in the Arab world:
that of *sex!*"
—*Reuters*
144 pp • $15.00 • 978-1-933372-68-6

Alberto Angela
A Day in the Life of Ancient Rome
"Fascinating and accessible."
—*Il Giornale*
392 pp • $16.00 • 978-1-933372-71-6

Muriel Barbery
The Elegance of the Hedgehog
"Gently satirical, exceptionally winning and inevitably bittersweet."
—Michael Dirda, *The Washington Post*
336 pp • $15.00 • 978-1-933372-60-0

Gourmet Rhapsody
"In the pages of this book, Barbery shows off her finest gift: lightness."
—*La Repubblica*
176 pp • $15.00 • 978-1-933372-95-2

Stefano Benni
Margherita Dolce Vita
"A modern fable…hilarious social commentary."—*People*
240 pp • $14.95 • 978-1-933372-20-4

Timeskipper
"Benni again unveils his Italian brand of magical realism."
—*Library Journal*
400 pp • $16.95 • 978-1-933372-44-0

Romano Bilenchi
The Chill
120 pp • $15.00 • 978-1-933372-90-7

Massimo Carlotto
The Goodbye Kiss
"A masterpiece of Italian noir."
—*Globe and Mail*
160 pp • $14.95 • 978-1-933372-05-1

Death's Dark Abyss
"A remarkable study of corruption and redemption."
—*Kirkus* (starred review)
160 pp • $14.95 • 978-1-933372-18-1

The Fugitive
"[Carlotto is] the reigning king of Mediterranean noir."
—*The Boston Phoenix*
176 pp • $14.95 • 978-1-933372-25-9

(with Marco Videtta)
Poisonville
"The business world as described by Carlotto and Videtta
in *Poisonville* is frightening as hell."
—*La Repubblica*
224 pp • $15.00 • 978-1-933372-91-4

Francisco Coloane
Tierra del Fuego
"Coloane is the Jack London of our times."—Alvaro Mutis
192 pp • $14.95 • 978-1-933372-63-1

Giancarlo De Cataldo
The Father and the Foreigner
"A slim but touching noir novel from one of Italy's best writers
in the genre."—*Quaderni Noir*
144 pp • $15.00 • 978-1-933372-72-3

Shashi Deshpande
The Dark Holds No Terrors
"[Deshpande is] an extremely talented storyteller."—*Hindustan Times*
272 pp • $15.00 • 978-1-933372-67-9

Helmut Dubiel
Deep In the Brain: Living with Parkinson's Disease
"A book that begs reflection."—*Die Zeit*
144 pp • $15.00 • 978-1-933372-70-9

Steve Erickson
Zeroville
"A funny, disturbing, daring and demanding novel—Erickson's best."
—*The New York Times Book Review*
352 pp • $14.95 • 978-1-933372-39-6

Elena Ferrante
The Days of Abandonment
"The raging, torrential voice of [this] author is something rare."
—*The New York Times*
192 pp • $14.95 • 978-1-933372-00-6

Troubling Love
"Ferrante's polished language belies the rawness of her imagery."
—*The New Yorker*
144 pp • $14.95 • 978-1-933372-16-7

The Lost Daughter
"So refined, almost translucent."—*The Boston Globe*
144 pp • $14.95 • 978-1-933372-42-6

Jane Gardam
Old Filth
"Old Filth belongs in the Dickensian pantheon of memorable characters."
—*The New York Times Book Review*
304 pp • $14.95 • 978-1-933372-13-6

The Queen of the Tambourine
"A truly superb and moving novel."—*The Boston Globe*
272 pp • $14.95 • 978-1-933372-36-5

The People on Privilege Hill
"Engrossing stories of hilarity and heartbreak."—*Seattle Times*
208 pp • $15.95 • 978-1-933372-56-3

The Man in the Wooden Hat
"Here is a writer who delivers the world we live in…with memorable and moving skill."—*The Boston Globe*
240 pp • $15.00 • 978-1-933372-89-1

Alicia Giménez-Bartlett
Dog Day
"Delicado and Garzón prove to be one of the more engaging sleuth teams to debut in a long time."—*The Washington Post*
320 pp • $14.95 • 978-1-933372-14-3

Prime Time Suspect
"A gripping police procedural."—*The Washington Post*
320 pp • $14.95 • 978-1-933372-31-0

Death Rites
"Petra is developing into a good cop, and her earnest efforts to assert her authority…are worth cheering."—*The New York Times*
304 pp • $16.95 • 978-1-933372-54-9

Katharina Hacker
The Have-Nots
"Hacker's prose soars."—*Publishers Weekly*
352 pp • $14.95 • 978-1-933372-41-9

Patrick Hamilton
Hangover Square
"Patrick Hamilton's novels are dark tunnels of misery, loneliness, deceit, and sexual obsession."—*New York Review of Books*
336 pp • $14.95 • 978-1-933372-06-

James Hamilton-Paterson
Cooking with Fernet Branca
"Irresistible!"—*The Washington Post*
288 pp • $14.95 • 978-1-933372-01-3

Amazing Disgrace
"It's loads of fun, light and dazzling as a peacock feather."
—*New York Magazine*
352 pp • $14.95 • 978-1-933372-19-8

Rancid Pansies
"Campy comic saga about hack writer and self-styled 'culinary genius' Gerald Samper."—*Seattle Times*
288 pp • $15.95 • 978-1-933372-62-4

Seven-Tenths: The Sea and Its Thresholds
"The kind of book that, were he alive now, Shelley might have written."
—*Charles Spawson*
416 pp • $16.00 • 978-1-933372-69-3

Alfred Hayes
The Girl on the Via Flaminia
"Immensely readable."—*The New York Times*
164 pp • $14.95 • 978-1-933372-24-2

Jean-Claude Izzo
Total Chaos
"Izzo's Marseilles is ravishing."—*Globe and Mail*
256 pp • $14.95 • 978-1-933372-04-4

Chourmo
"A bitter, sad and tender salute to a place equally impossible to love
or leave."—*Kirkus* (starred review)
256 pp • $14.95 • 978-1-933372-17-4

Solea
"[Izzo is] a talented writer who draws from the deep, dark well of noir."
—*The Washington Post*
208 pp • $14.95 • 978-1-933372-30-3

The Lost Sailors
"Izzo digs deep into what makes men weep."—*Time Out New York*
272 pp • $14.95 • 978-1-933372-35-8

A Sun for the Dying
"Beautiful, like a black sun, tragic and desperate."—*Le Point*
224 pp • $15.00 • 978-1-933372-59-4

Gail Jones
Sorry
"Jones's gift for conjuring place and mood rarely falters."
—*Times Literary Supplement*
240 pp • $15.95 • 978-1-933372-55-6

Matthew F. Jones
Boot Tracks
"A gritty action tale."—*The Philadelphia Inquirer*
208 pp • $14.95 • 978-1-933372-11-2

www.europaeditions.com

Ioanna Karystiani
The Jasmine Isle
"A modern Greek tragedy about love foredoomed and family life."
—*Kirkus*
288 pp • $14.95 • 978-1-933372-10-5

Swell
"Karystiani movingly pays homage to the sea and those who live from it."
—*La Repubblica*
256 pp • $15.00 • 978-1-933372-98-3

Gene Kerrigan
The Midnight Choir
"The lethal precision of his closing punches leave quite a lasting mark."
—*Entertainment Weekly*
368 pp • $14.95 • 978-1-933372-26-6

Little Criminals
"A great story...relentless and brilliant."—*Roddy Doyle*
352 pp • $16.95 • 978-1-933372-43-3

Peter Kocan
Fresh Fields
"A stark, harrowing, yet deeply courageous work of immense power and magnitude."—*Quadrant*
304 pp • $14.95 • 978-1-933372-29-7

The Treatment and the Cure
"Kocan tells this story with grace and humor."—*Publishers Weekly*
256 pp • $15.95 • 978-1-933372-45-7